Rural Costume

Its Origin and Development in Western
Europe and the British Isles

Rural Costume

*Its Origin and Development in Western
Europe and the British Isles*

ALMA OAKES and MARGOT HAMILTON HILL

B T Batsford Ltd   *London*
Van Nostrand Reinhold Company   *New York*

Filmset by Filmtype Services Ltd, Scarborough, Yorks
Printed by Billing & Sons, Guildford, Surrey
Bound by Hunter & Foulis, Edinburgh

Published in Great Britain by
B T Batsford Ltd
4 Fitzhardinge Street, London W 1 England
and in the United States of America by
Van Nostrand Reinhold Company
450 West 33rd Street, New York, New York 10001

16 15 14 13 12 11 10 9 8 7 6 5 4 3 2 1

391
011r

Contents

Acknowledgements

I would like to express my thanks to Mr. Donald King, Deputy Keeper, Department of Textiles, Victoria and Albert Museum for the great help and encouragement he gave me writing this book.

To Mr. Charles Gibbs-Smith, Keeper of the Department of Public Relations and Education of the Victoria and Albert Museum for his help and advice.

To Miss M. C. Watson and Miss Betty Greenhill of the Brighton Reference Library for their help in obtaining the books I needed, and to Mr. Ray, former Librarian of Horsham Public Library.

To Dr. van Daalen of the Zeeuws Museum, Middleburg, Netherlands.

To the Staff of the Information Office of the Folk Museum, Arnhem, Netherlands and Frü Bugge of the Folk Museum, Oslo for their help and interest.

My very grateful thanks to Miss Margaret Playle and Miss Sylvia Mann for their very careful editing and typing of my complicated manuscript.

Foreword

Books on the history of European costume generally concentrate on aristocratic and bourgeois fashions, which, because of their rapid rate of change, provide a graphic index to the ideals and fantasies of successive generations, successive decades, and even of successive years and seasons. The present book treats of a very different subject, that of rural dress, which followed a quite different timescale, since here the flux of fantasy was checked by practical considerations, by the slower rhythms of country life and the innate conservatism of country folk, perhaps by poverty, or by sumptuary laws, or the weight of local traditions. In its own way, however, rural dress was no less rich and varied than aristocratic and bourgeois dress. It could be extravagantly elaborate, and, though it evolved more slowly, it was apt to incorporate features of various periods in new and original ensembles. Moreover, while the costume of the upper and middle classes always tended to be rather international, rural costume was intensely regional, varying widely from country to country and even from village to village. Inevitably, modern social and economic developments, the spread of cheap and rapid transport and the techniques of instant communication, have destroyed the older patterns of country life, and traditional rural costume hardly survives in western Europe at the present time, save as a self-conscious archaism or an attraction for tourists.

The study of rural costume began as a by-product of the Romantic movement early in the nineteenth century and has continued to be inspired by romantic ideals of patriotism, both national and local. In view of the variety of local traditions it is indeed quite natural that rural costume should chiefly be studied on a national or regional basis. The writer of the present book first approached the subject in this way, through her interest in the regional costume of the Netherlands. Some years ago, however, she described to me her project for a work of a more comprehensive nature, a synoptic study of rural costume in western Europe and the British Isles, with reference not so much to the differences, as to the relationships, between the various regional traditions. I replied that, since rather little work had been done on this aspect of the subject, it seemed to me that the undertaking would probably be a difficult one, but that it might well prove eminently worth while. Boldly interpreting this as encouragement, Miss Oakes plunged into her self-appointed task, and the text of her book now lies before us. Though it naturally makes use of such publications as exist in this field, it is to a remarkable degree an original and independent work, based on many years of personal study and reflection. There can be few students of costume who will fail to find here many unfamiliar facts and ideas.

The carefully chosen illustrations, which form an indispensable adjunct to the text, have been ably redrawn by Miss Hamilton Hill from many original sources.

DONALD KING

Introduction

For many years I had the good fortune to live on the Dutch Island of Walcheren, and I can remember the time when the greater part of the farming community wore their most becoming and, in those days, fairly economical and durable dress. It was so pleasant to see the ingrained good taste, both in line and materials, that the wearers of traditional dress seemed to possess, as opposed to the lack of taste of their relatives and friends who preferred the cheap, ready-to-wear clothing that was sold in most countries before the Second World War: and I was impressed by the independence, courage and love of tradition of these people who dressed themselves differently from the majority of the human beings around them.

Most of the wearers of traditional dress disliked being stared at and photographed, as was inevitable when they were outside their own district. The idea that they donned the dress to attract tourists (with a few minor exceptions) is a complete fallacy. Even in such tourist places as Marken and Volendam the dress, with all its complicated tradition, was worn just the same in the touristless winter. That their unusual dress did attract tourists, however, is true, and this probably contributed to its survival. As a result of large-scale land reclamation, Marken will eventually become a farming instead of a fishing village, and this may lead to the disappearance of one of the oldest traditional dresses of western Europe.

There are, of course, disadvantages in the wearing of regional costume, especially when a new fashion encourages exaggerations. The dress is often restrictive and heavy, especially for children. This factor in the disappearance of regional dress was increased by the arrival of the comfortable, unrestricting post-1918 clothes worn by the majority. Another factor is the difficulty of obtaining the specially woven materials often needed, and their high cost when obtainable.

Although some articles of clothing and jewellery were handed on, there were never enough to go round. Then, too, young people did not want to wear "those old-fashioned things that belonged to Mother or Grandmother", but wanted the latest fashion in jewellery or dress details, since the basic items of the costume showed little change throughout the centuries. In Walcheren and other parts of the province of Zeeland – until recently one of the strongholds of regional dress – it is now scarcely ever worn by anybody under thirty years of age.

Marken, Volendam and Spakenburg, each with an individual dress, may retain it for a time, as it still is worn by the children. There are other small communities where it is still worn, though rarely by any young people. It is sad that within a short time something that has had such a long tradition, has always been flattering to the wearer and with time has acquired dignity and suitability, will have completely disappeared, except, as in France and some other countries, for fêtes and festivals.

Unfortunately, in the Netherlands, where the costume has managed to survive in spite of so many difficulties, when it is given up it is given up for good, and the often elaborate silver and gold jewellery is sold to buy an ordinary outfit; it is not even worn for special occasions that have any real connection with farm life. An exception is the lovely dress worn by Friesian ladies for special occasions – but that is not a *rural* costume.

In France most rural costumes have disappeared, and even in Brittany the dress is generally worn only for Pardons, fêtes and gatherings of the "folk" kind.

In Spain rural dresses are no longer worn by country people, except in Ibiza in the Balearic Isles. In Portugal one or two places still retain them.

In Italy regional costume is still worn by the women of Lucania and Calabria. In Lucania it is found chiefly in the villages north of Potenza and can be seen at the great annual Fair held at Rionero in August. In Calabria (in certain villages of the Sila) it can be seen worn by women of all ages at the daily market at Nicastro and in great variety at the Festival of San Francesco di Paola at Paola on May 2nd. It is also worn in Sardinia.

In Switzerland, where formerly the wearing of the dress was so strictly controlled, it is now worn only at "peasant gatherings", although only a few years ago in Evelone, a remote mountain village, regional costume was still generally worn. However, excellent books of photographs of such dresses are to be found in the possession of families and museums. The same applies to the Scandinavian countries, with one exception in both Norway and Denmark, and to Wales where the dress is only worn for singing festivals.

In Bavaria, regional dress is still worn at Grunwald, near Munich.

In Austria the becoming dirndl is derived from rural dresses. It is not traditional, but was created after 1918 as a national costume in remembrance of the ancient and lost Austrian Empire.

I shall try here to trace the beginnings of the rural dress and its development. Inevitably there will be gaps in such a huge subject; but I hope to arouse enough interest for others to fill in the gaps for themselves. I shall not give many details of dresses after 1830, unless they are part of a long tradition. There are many excellent books dealing with different aspects of regional costume in western Europe and even with English dress.

After the abolition of the sumptuary laws, following the French Revolution, regional costumes had a flowering which continued well into the nineteenth century. Illustrators and publishers, observing a new enthusiasm for nature and rural life, produced a spate of books on the regional costumes of many countries between 1809 and 1850. Unfortunately, though many of the illustrations are excellent and often very accurate, there is an almost complete lack of historical background in the text.

At the end of the nineteenth century, when it was realised that the regional costumes were disappearing, many more books appeared, and this time with historical information – as in Hottenroth's *Deutsche Volkstracht,* Vols I, II and III, a very interesting though complicated book on German peasant costume. Konrad Mautner has also published a reliable work on regional dresses in Germany (1932). In the twentieth century, and especially since 1940, the Scandinavian countries and the Netherlands have published excellent scholarly books devoted entirely to rural dress. A list of these books is given in the Bibliography.

I must be forgiven if, for reasons of clarity, some facts are repeated in various parts of the book. I shall give a short survey of the origins of costumes in various countries and then describe the basic garments. I hope to throw light on the question why the costume survived in some countries and disappeared in others.

Finally, a note on the apparent inconsistency in the spelling of particular garments. Since there are variations of nomenclature, large or small, from province to province, it seemed best not to impose an artificial uniformity where no real one exists.

1. Historical Survey
of the Development of Rural Dress

Men's clothing   _39_

Beginnings   _to pg._

(The costume of country people in western Europe varied very little
from that of the Greek shepherd and his family until the beginning of
the fifteenth century. The worker on the land was either a serf or
semi-serf with a tiny parcel of land for his own use. But both serf and
semi-serf, one tied to an overlord, the other a holder of rented land,
also had obligations to his landlord. Payment was in kind. The wives
usually had their share of land work; their homes, or rather hovels,
were small and dark, and there was little time for weaving or making
anything but the simplest clothes. The peasants' tunic, _tunique, fra_ or
"frock" was derived from the Greek _chiton_ and Roman _tunica,_ and for
many centuries showed scarcely any change. Though this garment
went by different names, I shall call it the tunic. The tunic was usually
worn belted, but most early illustrations show it worn loose for threshing and harvesting generally. It was made of coarse woven linen, hemp
or wool according to climate and such material as was to hand.)

(Under the tunic were worn short full drawers – _bracca, braies_ or
breeches, held up by a thong of leather or some other material threaded
through the top of the garment. According to Strutt this garment was
rarely worn by Greek or Roman peasants, but was known to them.
The Gauls, the early Germans and Spanish workers wore long straight
Celtic trews or trousers; early Spanish mural paintings show them
with coloured checks. The Goths had often a "dagged" (i.e. notched)
edge to their trews, probably to prevent them from fraying, and they
were tied below the knee, a custom that was still seen among farm
workers in England in the twentieth century. Sometimes strips of
material were used to bind the legs, but usually the trews reached to the
calf or ankle. Although mostly worn until the early fifteenth century
in northern countries, they eventually developed all over western
Europe into knee breeches and then full-length trousers.

For winter wear and for journeys, a short cloak was worn, often with
a hood. This cloak, according to Cunnington, was derived from the
ninth- or tenth-century French _Saga Tressonica._

1. SPAIN, *c.* 1100: Catalonia. Poor man. Brown woven cloak. Red ochre tunic and *terre verte* trousers. (Unesco Book)

2. BRITISH ISLES, mid-thirteenth century: England. (Rutland Psalter)

3. FRANCE, *c.* 1270. Threshing Corn. (Jean Porcher)

4. BOHEMIA, *c.* 1350. Sowing. These corn-holding cloths were very general in the fourteenth and fifteenth centuries. (Velislav Bible)

In Spain the early rural cloak was more akin to the Roman shepherd's mantle, full, long, and fastened on one shoulder. The "rugged" mantle of the Scandinavian and Celtic countries is of very ancient origin and varies little in shape, colour and material from one found in a Danish Bronze Age tomb. The material is coarse wool of a very dark natural colour; it is long, circular, and fastened in front with two round ornaments connected by a chain.

Coarse woollen materials and skins with the leather worn outside were used for the hooded cloaks which were worn continuously in many countries for several centuries. They were in some cases shortened to become a shoulder cape.

For protection against the sun in summer, coarsely woven straw hats were worn; sometimes they were coolie shaped, sometimes they had a definite crown. The pointed, Phrygian-style Saxon cap, which fitted the head snugly, remained a favourite for all time, ending up as the fisherman's tasselled cap.

Hose were mostly rolled over at the tops, were knee-length or else tied just below the knee.

Shoes were ankle high, made of leather or cloth, with wooden soles or single soles like moccasins. Short ankle-boots of cowhide, or oxhide, or leather were also worn. Solid wooden shoes were probably used, but are seldom identifiable until the end of the fifteenth century. After the great plagues of the fourteenth century there was more freedom for rural people and the standard of living slowly improved, though serfdom persisted in some European countries until the French Revolution.

(Fifteenth century)

In western Europe a middle class was growing rapidly. Enclosed in walled towns, they developed a dress of their own, distinct from that of royalty and the nobility. It was this town dress which influenced the dress of the rural community, though often with a considerable time lag. The phenomenon of the town dress is most interesting. It is often recorded, and it persisted amongst women in the Netherlands, Germany, Switzerland and, to a lesser extent, in France and Italy. It is often confused with the rural dress and would be a worth-while subject for research.

By the middle of the fifteenth century men's dress in western Europe began slowly to imitate the more elaborate costume of the developing middle class. The belted tunic, formerly split from the waist downwards was now split from the neck to just above the knee; it was usually

5. FRANCE, 1416. The deliberately cut knee-holes and jagged edges to the trousers are noteworthy. *(Les Très Riches Heures du Duc de Berry)*

6. NORTH NETHERLANDS, *c.* 1428-45. (Hours of Catherine of Cleves)

7. FRANCE, 1416. The harvesting dress in a warm climate. *(Les Très Riches Heures du Duc de Berry)*

8. BRITISH ISLES, 1340: England. (Luttrell Psalter)

18

collarless but had revers, and took the form of the jerkin-jacket. The loose tunic-frock did not disappear entirely; it was still used in the warmer countries for working in the fields.

The Italians seem to have adopted the belted jerkin earlier than most countries. In the northern countries a short tunic with sleeves and split at the sides was worn under the jerkin, but in southern countries this was not general. Eventually all tunics were tucked into the breeches or trousers and became the shirt.

Short, fairly wide breeches, more shaped than the *braies* or under-drawers were worn; in Flanders, Ireland and Denmark, however, the long, narrow trews or trousers of the Gauls still persisted, though they were better cut. With breeches, rolled or tied hose were worn. The higher boot with turned-over top appeared in Italy in 1460, in Germany in 1470 and in Spain in 1529, but strapped or laced shoes, some with wooden soles or made like moccasins with a strong leather sole, were more generally worn. In Spain the roped *espadrille* or laced sandal was used in the early sixteenth century; this was probably introduced by the Moors.

Headgear became more varied and important from the end of the fourteenth century. The coif with a *lirripipe*, a long pointed end which could be wound round the hood of the cloak to keep it in place, was copied from a fashionable mode. In all countries the most typical hat was round with a medium-high crown, with a brim which was some-times turned up all round, sometimes up in front and down at the back for protection from the sun. The straw hat was still worn, but was slightly different in shape from the previous centuries, higher in the crown and less like a coolie hat. The high Phrygian-Saxon hood contin-ued to be a favourite. Towards the end of the fifteenth century and well into the sixteenth century the loose, full jerkin reached to just above the knee, always belted and with an opening which formed revers and showed the undergarment worn with or without a collar. When the bourgeois jerkin fashion was followed, the sleeves were narrow and tight; when it was purely rural the sleeves were full and loose.

The full jerkin, with the open revers neck was in general use amongst the rural population of the whole of western Europe and England; this is astonishing considering how little contact the rural populations can have had with each other.

There seems to have been no regional dress at this period. This was probably due to the fact that the various countries in Europe were constantly being invaded, over-run and settled by neighbours or near neighbours. That would not apply to England. Only Ireland had its own costume (until conquest by England) and the very isolated parts of Wales.

9. FRANCE, 1416. Swineherd. *(Les Très Riches Heures du Duc de Berry)*

10. FRANCE, late fifteenth century. An early straw hat and footless stockings. (Tapestry, Musée des Arts Decoratifs)

11. FRANCE, *c.* 1490. (Hours of Charles d'Angoulême. Bib. Nat.)

12. FRANCE, *c.* 1490. Country Dance. (Hours of Charles d'Angoulême. Bib. Nat.)

Materials, however, were regional: there were more woollen garments in some countries, more hempen, coarse linen and cotton cloth in others. Dyes, and therefore colours, varied according to which plants grew locally. Seafaring and wealthier countries imported indigo and cochineal. As the sixteenth century advanced both blue and red from these imported dyes were used in rural clothing.

Sixteenth century

In the fifteenth and the following century the fairly tight material hose was still worn under the loose belted jerkin, though knee length, fairly tight breeches were worn in the sixteenth century in Spain and Italy, and were the forerunners of the very baggy garments, the "slops" of the seventeenth century. Also in the sixteenth century Dutch seamen introduced a new fashion – long, straight, full trousers that could be easily rolled up for working purposes. This type of trouser was worn in the Scandinavian countries, the Faroes and other Danish islands, and, according to Hottenroth, influenced the northern part of Germany. Shoes, high and low, and the short boots did not vary very much until the seventeenth century; then the high boot with the big turn-over flap, occasionally seen at the end of the sixteenth century, became far more generally worn.

As usual, the big variation was in the headgear. At the end of the fifteenth century the hooded cape, sometimes dagged, was still fairly general in all countries. Sometimes it was topped by a round, shallow brimmed felt hat. Hats became more usual in the sixteenth century; they were mostly small with high, low or flat crowns, with the brim turned up or down, occasionally ornamented with a feather, and this type of hat, together with the Phrygian-Saxon hood, remained in use for a considerable time. In seafaring countries the seamen, especially in the Netherlands, wore for the first time at the end of the sixteenth century a high coif of rough, shaggy fur, the prototype of those seen today in Volendam and the Island of Urk. Towards the end of the sixteenth century the brim began to widen and the crown to rise, until the wide-brimmed hat which followed a bourgeois fashion appeared in the seventeenth century and became general in all countries.

It was the sixteenth century, however, which showed the greatest diversity of headgear, nor was this confined to any one country. It was in this century that the rural peoples of western Europe and England were better dressed than in the previous and following centuries. This is made apparent by the numerous sumptuary laws of this period forbidding the wearing of rich materials and gold and silver ornaments.

13. SPAIN, 1529. Castilian Shepherd. Some sort of bag sling is attached to the strap. (Weiditz)

14. BOHEMIA, 1520. (Lucas van Leyden. Rijksmuseum)

15. SPAIN, 1529. Corn Thresher. (Weiditz)

16. SPAIN, 1529. Moriscoes. The sandals (*espadrilles*) are still worn in Spain. (Weiditz)

17. SOUTH NETHERLANDS, 1559-63. (Breughel)

18. SOUTH NETHERLANDS, 1564. The shirt is
   visible below the jacket. (Breughel)

19. SOUTH NETHERLANDS, 1559-63. (Breughel)

20. SOUTH NETHERLANDS, 1564. The bottle is for
water, the box for bread. (Breughel)

21. SOUTH NETHERLANDS, 1559. (Breughel)

22. SOUTH NETHERLANDS, 1568. (Breughel)

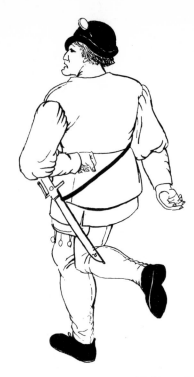

23. SOUTH NETHERLANDS, 1566. (Breughel)

24. SOUTH NETHERLANDS, 1565. (Breughel)

25. SOUTH NETHERLANDS, c. 1568. The 'Pipes' player. He wears a sword. South Netherlands and German peasants were allowed to wear swords as a protection in lawless times. (Breughel)

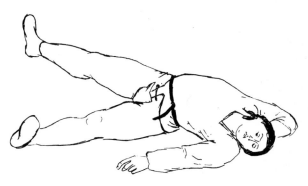

26. SOUTH NETHERLANDS, 1570. The cap is derived from an early bourgeois model. The breeches ties are loosened for digging. (Breughel)

27. SOUTH NETHERLANDS, 1565. Resting after harvesting. (Breughel)

28. FRANCE, 1567. 'Le Laboureur'. (Recueil de Paris)

29. FRANCE, 1567. 'Le Champenoys'. This farmer is carrying a basket of cheeses resting on straw. (Recueil de Paris)

30. GERMANY, sixteenth century: Lower Rhine-
land. The breeches are akin to those of German
Switzerland in the early nineteenth century.
(Hottenroth)

31. FRANCE, 1581. (de Bruyn)

32. DENMARK, 1580. (Ellen Andersen)

33. DENMARK, 1612: From Sildea, an island near
the Faroes. Note the deliberate cut in right
elbow; the right arm uses the sickle and the
scythe. (Georgius Braun. *Atlas*)

Seventeenth century

The seventeenth century brought devastating wars in Europe, and in England the effects of land enclosure were beginning to be felt by the peasants.

With the exception of the Netherlands, documentation and illustration of rural costume in the seventeenth century is difficult to find. Artists in the Netherlands were concerned chiefly with the wealthy middle class and the fairly well-to-do farmers and their dependants, but not in general with the nobility, whereas in other countries the artists' interest was either romantic or fashionable. The artists' subjects were painted in classical or romantic style and portraiture was of people of importance.

In Italy, France and Spain there was a tendency on the part of the artists, especially towards the middle of the century, to accentuate the romantic poverty of the rural people and their costume; and it is certain that the constant and lengthy wars greatly worsened the conditions of the peasants in many western European countries; this is very noticeable in their clothing.

The first signs of regional dress now became apparent, as well as a difference between the clothing of the wealthy farmer and the much poorer farm labourer. The costume seems seldom to have been regional to small, limited areas, but rather regional according to district. Elaboration of detail depended on the prosperity of a particular district. There is also greater variety in the popular jerkin. In the more agriculturally prosperous northern countries, a heavier type of material was used, the garment was looser and fuller, the basque of the jerkin more deeply pleated. Following the bourgeois fashion the sleeves were set in low on the shoulder though the sixteenth-century roll was retained: this roll held the shoulder and the arm seams together and remained a mark of rural dress well into the eighteenth century. The jerkin, when hip-length, was usually belted, and in all countries the fifteenth century revers were retained, to which was added a small, neat turn-down collar. Details like the sixteenth-century small ruff persisted well into the seventeenth century.

A straight, loose and unbelted jacket, either to the waist or just below, is often illustrated. The old tunic having become the shirt, the frock reappeared in a new form as a protection to clothing for working purposes.

Breeches were now usual; the full, round baggy Dutch slops, knee-length, were generally worn. But in France the breeches were straight, though full, and reached to slightly below the knee. The same type lasted well into the eighteenth century, but by then mostly had knee slits with buttons and buttonholes. In the rural dress the slits

34. NORTH NETHERLANDS, seventeenth century.
A Dutch farmer in working dress. An early form
of yarks is used to bind the trousers. (Pieter
Aartsen, Budapest Museum)

35. DENMARK, 1674: Amager, early Dutch-
Danish. (Holder Jacobaeus)

36. BRITISH ISLES, seventeenth century: England.
The English slops. (Roxburghe Ballads)

37. NORTH NETHERLANDS, c. 1720. Fishermen of
Marken. The costume looks 100 years earlier. The
'slops' remained unchanged until modern times in
Holland. (P. v. d. Berge)

were practically always left open, whereas in the bourgeois knee breeches they were usually closed. Long, straight trousers were also worn in northern countries in the seventeenth century; they were more like modern trousers than trunk hose.

High leather boots with big turnovers were worn in northern countries, though low shoes, with and without flaps, often tied in front, and mostly with low heels, were more popular. One picture of about 1600 shows the sole of the shoe with a circle of nails. Probably many shoes were like this, but the soles are rarely illustrated. The strap shoe was still worn, but not as often as formerly.

The headgear, too, shows great variation. There is one innovation – the big straw or felt hat. It has a medium-sized crown, flat or round and indented, with a wide brim turned up at the back or front. It was a useful all-weather hat, and a working copy of the gentlemen's plumed elegance. This large, rather floppy style survived until the nineteenth century, when it was superseded by a modified top hat. The Phrygian-Saxon type, pointed, high crowned hat, mostly with a narrow brim, was also worn in nearly all countries. In the northern Netherlands and parts of Denmark the furred hat already mentioned was worn in the more rounded form seen so often in Dutch seventeenth-century pictures. This is still worn.

The short cloak of the two preceding centuries was not worn by rural people, in fact there are few signs of men's cloaks at this time, except in Spain and France, where they were generally worn long and fastened at the neck.

Eighteenth century onward

The eighteenth-century countrymen adopted a fashion based on bourgeois dress which was to have a permanent influence on rural costume, and this fashion still survives in most countries where the dress is still worn.

At the beginning of the eighteenth century older people still wore the baggy breeches, the rather loose jerkins or jackets with the low set-in sleeves, and the floppy hats.

The men's dress in eighteenth-century Spain, then a very poor country, shows very little tendency to follow the fashion of the day, even with the long gap that always occurs before rural people adopt a bourgeois fashion. Nevertheless, there are records of a very early regional dress, fifteenth-century, based on a bourgeois fashion, which survived into the early nineteenth century.

By the middle of the eighteenth century the majority of the rural

38. NORTH NETHERLANDS, 1693. A smart farmer with the long redingote type of coat. (From a stained glass portrait of Dirck van der Poel)

39. SPAIN, probably eighteenth century. Note the early type of bourgeois sleeveless coat. (Palencia)

40. NORWAY, eighteenth century. (Lexow)

41. FRANCE, eighteenth century. A peasant of the Angoumois. (St. Sauveur)

population had adopted the better cut long skirted jacket with numerous buttons and buttonholes. These jackets were waisted, had small turned-back revers, and reached to just below the hips. As the century advanced the long, full skirted jacket or coat appeared, with a modest collar and wider revers.

With the improvement in the financial position of the countryman a new garment came to fashion, a buttoned waistcoat of fashionable origin: a shirt was worn under the waistcoat. Breeches became tighter, though never fashionably tight. Sometimes they had simple ties and at other times unbuttoned slits, though the buttons themselves were there. The working dress consisted of shirt and breeches, or in some colder countries a loose tunic of thick material, like the knee-length seventeenth-century garment which now became waist-length and resembled the Jersey or Guernsey.

The hat at the beginning of this century retained the large floppy form of the previous century and continued to do so in France and southern European countries until, in the middle of the nineteenth century, the round hard felt hat with turned-up brim took its place. In the more northerly countries and Great Britain the big hat and bourgeois tricorne were worn for best. In the Netherlands and in parts of Denmark the seventeenth-century furred hat was worn by some fishermen and began to show a regional fashion, low in some places and high in others.

In Scandinavian countries, the Phrygian-Saxon type cap, pulled down tight against the cold, was the dominant style. In Italy and southern France it became the tasselled cap of the fisherman. For those who shot or hunted in cold weather, the fourteenth-century type of hooded cape was worn in countries as far apart as Spain and Denmark, and continued to be worn until the nineteenth century.

By this time men's headgear had become regional.

Shoes did not change very much in the eighteenth century; the majority wore the laced shoe or the low laced boot with leathern or wooden heels. High boots were worn with turnovers and in Scandinavia with wide openings without flaps. In the Netherlands, France and Germany the wooden shoe was used for work, and in Germany it sometimes had a wooden heel in the centre. In Spain it was mounted on four pegs – a feature with ancient origins. In England men wore thick leather shoes or boots, apparently only women wore the wooden patter or clog. In mountainous countries like Spain and Switzerland the *espadrille* and laced sandal was used. For best, and well into the nineteenth century, the leather shoe with silver or metal buckles and turn-back flaps was worn. Towards the end of the eighteenth century gaiters were worn in Scandinavia, Belgium, Germany and England.

42. NORWAY, eighteenth century. Oarsman from
Kloeboe. (Lexow)

43. FRANCE, eighteenth century. From the
Bordeaux area. (St. Sauveur)

44. NORWAY, eighteenth century. Woodman from
Horsanger. (Lexow)

45 FRANCE, eighteenth century. Peasant from the
Limoges district. (St. Sauveur)

46. ITALY, 1796: Tuscany. A typical Italian silk scarf, such as is still worn, is round the waist. (*Abito de Contadini Sposi*)

47. SPAIN, 1799: Santander. A seller of cloth. The cummerband or sash is of the type so much worn by rural men in many of the West European countries. The breeches turned up to show underpants and *espadrille* type of shoe. (Pasiego)

48. SPAIN, 1799: Jaen. Money bags are on the cummerband or sash. (*Colección General de Los Trages de España, 1799*)

49. SPAIN, 1799: Galicia. (*Colección General de Los Trages de España, 1799*)

50. NORWAY, c. 1800. (From a contemporary water-colour, private collection)

51. NORWAY, c. 1800. Blue cloth coat. Yellow under coat. White waistcoat. Dark blue cloth breeches. Brown garters with red turn over. Brown shoes. Blue cap. (From a contemporary water-colour, private collection)

52. NORTH NETHERLANDS, 1803-5. Black cloth coat with silver buttons. Brocaded waistcoat in various colours with silver buttons. Knee band with rosettes. Silver buckles on shoes. Black hat. Gold or silver buttons on neck handkerchief.

53. SWISS, 1815: Berne. Man with his milking equipment. The slashed breeches are typical of the lower Rhineland and German Switzerland. (Josy) (Koenig)

54. DUTCH-DANISH, early nineteenth century:
Amager (Mygdal)

55. DUTCH-DANISH, early nineteenth century:
Amager. Sunday or festival costume.
(Rieters Stik)

56. ITALY, 1914. Striped linen trousers held on by
cummerband or sash. (Costello, *Terra di larno el
Regno di Napoli*)

57. DUTCH-DANISH, early nineteenth century:
Amager. The dress that came with North
Netherlands farmers in the early seventeenth
century and remained unchanged until it disappeared. Fur hats were dyed blue (Mygdal)

35

58. SWITZERLAND, 1815. Cowherd from Appenzell.
(Josy) (Koenig)

59. SWITZERLAND, 1815. The old Swiss dress from
Mürren. The black cloth coat is edged with red
ribbon. Long trousers are attached to the belt by
double or treble corded bows. (Josy) (Koenig)

60. SPAIN, 1825. Goatherd of the environs of
Valladolid. Sheep or goatskin jacket and pouch.
(Ackermann)

61. ITALY, 1826. The sheepskin coat is noteworthy.
(F. Ferrari, *Raccolta di Costumi dello Stato
Romano*)

62. SWEDEN, 1823. From Herrestad Harad. (Forssell)

63. ITALY, 1826. The coloured silk scarf round the waist is typical. Breeches with open placket were usually worn by rural men. (Ferrari)

64. FRANCE, 1865: Brittany. The slops resemble those of the North Netherlands. (Darjou)

65. SARDINIA, nineteenth century. This dress was worn until recently and still is for folk festivals. (After a photograph)

66. DENMARK, nineteenth century. The short
    bourgeois-type coat is of the type favoured by
    nineteenth-century northern European rural men.
    The high hat was also worn in Scandinavia and in
    Zeeland (Netherlands) in the latter part of
    the nineteenth and early twentieth centuries.
    Ornamental waistcoats were general in western
    Europe in the eighteenth, nineteenth and twen-
    tieth centuries. (After a photograph)

67. NETHERLANDS, nineteenth century

68. FRANCE, 1865. Breton dress from Finistère.
    (Darjou)

38

Women's dress

Beginnings

The dress of rural women in the early twelfth and thirteenth centuries consisted of a long, simple gown, with bodice and skirt in one piece, made from two straight pieces sewn together, with long narrow sleeves to the wrist and without shoulder seams. This gown varied little from those of the ladies of the nobility except that the rural dress was untrimmed.

The neck opening in the earlier centuries was usually V-shaped and laced. A girdle held the garment in place, and over the girdle the gown could be drawn up and looped over, so making it easier to work in. In Italy and France the gowns illustrated in the early manuscripts are usually white and were probably woven of coarse linen or hemp. In the northern countries the dress is darker and of heavier materials.

Fourteenth-sixteenth centuries

In the early fourteenth century the bodice part of the gown became more shaped, and in the Luttrell Psalter it is sometimes shown covered by a garment resembling the *cote* of more fashionable women. As the century advanced the neck line varied and was worn oval, round or square. Bodice openings were sometimes laced to the waist and in Italy in some cases they were opened to form revers and to show the smock. The gowns themselves were more shaped, and a girdle was now not always necessary. In France and Italy the bodice fitted more closely. Aprons were worn over the gowns. Hottenroth reproduces a Gaulish sculpture of a country-woman wearing one, but they were not in general use until the fifteenth century. These aprons were and remained long and narrow for a considerable period.

In *Les Très Riches Heures du Duc de Berry* (1416) a gown makes its appearance with the upper part definitely having the cut of a bodice. It had a round-shaped neck, with a V opening which was laced. When the bodice had a front opening to the waist it was close-fastened, probably with a cord. Occasionally the bodice took the form of a short coat with sleeves set low on the shoulder; they are sometimes fitting and long; when short they show the sleeve of the smock.

This type of bodice became in some countries one of the basic garments of the rural women's costume, and remained so until the costume disappeared.

At the end of the fifteenth century the bodice was lengthened until it became a long jacket, such as was worn in Flanders and can be seen in Breughel's paintings. It also became more tailored and had a straight

69. DENMARK, third and first century B.C. Skirt of the Bronze Age period. (Köhler, *History of Costume*)

70. FRANCE, mid-fourteenth century. The influence of the wimple, which was to persist in rural dress. (Morgan Library)

71. ITALY, fourteenth century. Herb gatherers. An early double sleeve. *(Tacuinum Sanitatis)*

72. ITALY, fourteenth century. Herb gatherers. *(Tacuinum Sanitatis)*

back seam and curved side seams. These seams were also used in some French bodices of an earlier period, and the effect was often obtained not by cutting but by folding the seams and stitching them with firm but large stitches, so allowing for a "let out". These three back seams are still used in the bodices of the Zeeland peasant dresses.

From the end of the fifteenth century, for at least a hundred years, the closed bodice with a deep square opening, edged with a band, imitating a bourgeois fashion, was worn. The low opening was filled in by the smock or with a kerchief the point of which hung down the back of the bodice, a fashion which never departed from the rural dress. The opening was also filled in by a piece of material, sometimes round, and later on in the sixteenth century ended in a raised or open collar. This was very much worn in the Netherlands and Germany, and had many names; in the eighteenth century these names became regional.

An unusual wood-carving of a group of four peasant figures (1490) in Utrecht's Bischoplijk Museum gives a very good idea of these bodices. One has a pointed opening instead of the more usual square one, a band edges the bust opening, and the bodice has another feature which still survives – short lapels or basque which cover the upper part of the skirt. The sleeves are long. One carved figure is seen from the back and shows the pointed kerchief ending in a deep V.

The sleeves of this type of bodice were often short, showing the smock sleeves. The sleeves of the Dutch, Flemish, German and English bodices were on the whole narrower and longer than the French or Italian or Spanish. All countries wore at times the double sleeve, that is, a loose top sleeve with a tighter under one; or a loose sleeve attached by various methods to the shoulder or else to the elbow sleeve. The latter, however, was more often worn with the sleeveless corset-bodice which will be described next.

In the early sixteenth century there appeared the garment which I will call a corset-bodice, though the words used in the northern countries were variations of *stiklief,* meaning "enfolded, or encasing the body". This corset was boned, had either a pointed or square base, and was usually laced down the front over a wide opening; if back-laced, the opening was narrower. This garment is of royal derivation, being first worn by Queen Marie of Anjou in the middle of the fifteenth century. As a fashionable garment it was short-lived, but as a rural garment it has persisted down the centuries.

There are two types of corset-bodice, the very deep pointed type which as a rule has a rounded top and often sleeves, and was related to the French *basquin,* derived from a Spanish court garment. The other corset-bodice was square both at the base and top, with a wide opening and generally no sleeves, and was worn over the tight *placard* or

73. ITALY, fourteenth century. The Italian scarf remained with the costume until the twentieth century. *(Tacuinum Sanitatis)*

74. ITALY, fourteenth century. A typical 'veil' headdress as used by Roman women. *(Tacuinum Sanitatis)*

75. FRANCE, *c.* 1405-10. (Porcher)

76. ITALY, fourteenth century. An early form of gown opening, and bag attached to a cord. *(Tacuinum Sanitatis)*

partlet or front, or – in southern counties and Flanders, for example – over a loose white smock. Detachable sleeves were mostly worn with this garment, except during work. Falling ruffs were occasionally worn with both bodice and corset-bodice, but always in conjunction with the partlet and not the smock. The kerchief was even more rarely worn with the corset-bodice in the sixteenth century, though often with the closed bodice. When the skirt and bodice ceased to be one, as they probably did in the late fifteenth century, the skirt became a separate garment. It was, and remained, a strictly practical garment for working women, and throughout the centuries did not vary very much. In all countries it was full and considerably shorter than the bourgeois fashion, though in most cases it did reach to the ankles. A. J. Holbein's engraving of 1500 shows a fashionable skirt with one band of velvet on the hem and another just above it. This fashion was adopted by many countrywomen; it is found in England, Germany, France and especially Italy. The band on the hem was found to give it durability and the second band above may have been used to hide a let-down seam or purely for decoration. Anyhow, these bands, sometimes becoming three or four, remained throughout the centuries as a mark of rural costume, especially the gala dress.

The apron came into general use in the sixteenth century, probably because the skirt could not be so easily pulled under and over the girdle for protection as the gown.

The aprons were wider than those worn in the previous centuries usually without bibs. There were apparently two kinds of aprons, and both are illustrated in the early sixteenth-century Flemish *Heures de Notre Dame de Hennessey*[1] miniature for the month of August. The old woman wears a piece of white linen or hemp, which hung down in front, and the top was cut so that it could be tied behind. A younger woman also wears a white apron, but this is of finer pleated material and is gathered into a narrow band, forming strings and tied behind. Both types of apron were worn in most countries. Sometimes they were made of wool and canvas and were blue and red in colour, and in 1600 black cloth is mentioned, but white was more general in the sixteenth century.

The Italian gala apron was already at this period an elaborate and embroidered affair, though not made of heavy materials like those used in the eighteenth and nineteenth centuries.

The cloak was the generally recognised rural garment in Europe. From the earliest centuries it was a simple circular affair made from dark natural wool like the prehistoric garment recovered from a Danish tomb. The early Irish and Welsh mantles were like this and were used for day-wear and night blanket. The poor Irish peasant women wore them sometimes loose, sometimes belted. The full-belted mantle

1. Flanders, 1520

77. NORTH NETHERLANDS, c. 1450 (Hours of
Catherine of Cleves)

78. SOUTH NETHERLANDS, 1481. An unusual
shaped gown showing the shift. Loose sleeves.
(Breviary in the Mayer van den Bergh collection,
Antwerp)

79 FRANCE, fifteenth century: An early straw
rural hat and a typical turn-up of over-dress. (*Le
Livre des Saisons*)

80. GERMANY, mid-fifteenth century. Alsatian
straw hat. Deep blue gown with red lining. White
wimple. Blue and white check under petticoat.
White socks. Red shoes. (Tapestry, Victoria and
Albert Museum)

somewhat resembled the *huik*, an interesting garment described separately.

The cloak was obviously used by women to go to market, especially in winter. The *Heures de Notre Dame de Hennessey* winter scene shows a woman in a shapeless fawn cloak draped over her head and under her arms, and pulled round the body. Another example of cloak shown is hooded. These shapeless garments were at this period worn for protection in bad weather, but later on they became straighter and fuller and more often hooded, and remained a distinctive rural garment until the twentieth century.

Italian rural women do not seem to have worn the cloak; they used a scarf or shawl. In contrast, the wealthy women of Spain were enveloped in black mantles for outdoor wear; these survived in most countries as a rural mourning garment.

Stockings in the early centuries, when worn, were covered by the gown, the shoe only being visible. They probably resembled those of the bourgeois women, being of material and sewn up the back. The texture of those worn by the countrywoman would be coarse and hard-wearing.

The shoes resembled those of the men and followed the pattern of a primitive shoe made of a rectangular piece of skin folded up over the foot and then fastened with a thong drawn through a row of holes placed close together along the free edges of the skin. This simple type of shoe was used in Denmark in the bronze age and was the foot gear of the peasant in Roman times. It is still worn in Dalecarlia in Sweden and until recently in Runo, the Faroe Islands and Iceland.[1]

In many of the early illustrations this shoe comes to well above the ankles and has a rolled turnover, and apparently no fastening.

By the sixteenth century many countries had a shoe with a wooden or cork sole. The Germans wore a short boot, so did the Alsatians. The Spaniards and Italians had a sandal-type shoe with wooden soles.

Nearly all countries seem to have used the patten, *galoche* or *pantouffle*, soled wooden shoes or over-shoes, usually with a strap of leather, no back but with a slight heel; these were used by country-women for outdoor wear, especially in the winter. The pattens also had cork soles, but these were probably worn by wealthier women, as were also the high wooden Spanish *zapota* or *choppino*, which Weiditz illus-trates as being worn as far apart as Limousin and Ireland. Some sort of protection against the muddy lanes of those days must have been needed. All the shoes of the rural women were heelless, better to accommodate the patten. I have not found any women wearing the deeply hollowed-out wooden sabot at this period.

The rural head-dress was and still is the most important part of the

1. R. Blonguist; *Kulturen*, 1943

45

81. FRANCE, *c.* 1490. Country dance. (Hours of Charles d'Angoulême)

82. FRANCE, *c.* 1490 (Hours of Charles d'Angoulême)

83. FRANCE, 1486. Village Woman. (Pierre le Rouge)

whole costume. It was the first of the garments to have a special meaning. It would denote region, status (married or unmarried), form of religion, and very often age. Other garments often closely followed the bourgeois mode but, very early on, the rural head-dress in Europe differed far more from that of the wealthier women than any other item of the costume. The differentiation of rural and upper class headgear was even occasionally enforced. For instance, in Switzerland the lower orders in the sixteenth century and probably earlier were compelled by degree to wear the *Tuchli,* a kind of wimple coif.

The earliest type of head-dress for rural women was the linen hood, open in front, with long pointed ends covering the ears and a long end falling down the back, probably made from a triangular piece of material. This type of hood was worn in Italy, France, the Netherlands and England in the fourteenth century, probably by older women, and it is often a sign of widowhood. Simultaneously in these countries, a round fitting coif was worn by younger women. Unmarried girls went bareheaded.

Hottenroth illustrates Gaulish women wearing bands of linen swathed round the head and forming side pieces. A similar head-dress was worn by Irish women in the sixteenth century. The kerchief simply fastened under the chin with a long back was worn in the late fifteenth century in the Netherlands; and a rolled linen head-dress with long ends, leaving the face free, dates from the same period.

In Spain the head-dress when first recorded is different from that of other parts of Europe. It was a curious turban shape rising to a point with a *forward* bend, and this, with various other examples worn in the Basque country, seems to show a Moorish influence. It is the first indication of a regional coif. Though the wimple-type coif was worn in Spain, as well as in most western European countries, in general the Spanish head-dress was of a very different origin and type.

In the sixteenth century far more rural costumes are recorded and it is much easier to study the various influences. There are probably four principal ones, the wimple and the *henin,* the *bongrace* combined with coif, and the high pointed Phrygian-Saxon type coif. The more tight-fitting coif, with a winged effect was not worn much before the end of the sixteenth century and the beginning of the seventeenth, the country of origin probably being the Netherlands, where starching of cuffs and coifs was first invented about 1560.

The wimple coif predominated, especially in north-western Europe and could still be seen in Norway in 1840. In England it seems to have been rarely worn by countrywomen. The *henin*-type coif was not worn in England by rural women, but a moderate *henin* shaped like a barrel with a flat top, consisting of a frame covered with a piece of material draped

84. GERMANY, 1517. (Altdorfer)

85. GERMANY, 1517. The straw hat and apron are rural. The wimple and double sleeve show bourgeois influence. (Altdorfer)

86. SPAIN, 1529. Basque woman wearing typical Basque headdress. (Weiditz)

87. SPAIN, 1529. A Spanish apron of a type which is also found in Sardinia. (Weiditz)

round and over the top leaving a hanging end, appears in illustrations from Navarre, Brittany and Germany in the first half of the sixteenth century, and it survived in various forms in the Breton coif.

The *bongrace* was a bourgeois fashion in the first quarter of the sixteenth century. It consisted of a piece of material folded flat on the head and attached to a tight coif. It was adopted by the rural people and seems to have become part of the coif. A Flemish peasant in a picture by Mathys wears it, and a French engraving of 1575 in the Louvre also shows one. However, it was the Italian countrywomen who really adopted this style of head-dress. Hollar in a 1643 engraving of a woman of *Matriciana* in the Abruzzi gives the clearest idea of this head-dress. By the nineteenth century it might almost be called a national head-dress, probably because it was an excellent protection against the sun.

The fourth type of coif was the Phrygian-Saxon style coif, up to the sixteenth century worn only by men. I cannot trace the exact period when women adopted this fashion. It appears in a Danish costume in the seventeenth century, but probably went to that country from West Friesland with the Dutch-Amager people at the end of the sixteenth century. There are engravings of it in West Friesland at the end of the seventeenth century. Spanish women also were fond of a pointed coif which may have influenced the Dutch women. The pointed coif fitting tightly to the head was much worn in Norway in the eighteenth and early nineteenth century and it is still worn as an under cap by Volendam woman beneath their white coifs, also high pointed and winged, but these are being discarded in favour of the under cap only. The shaped coif, usually white, framing the face with narrow lace or frill as seen in the *Heures de Notre Dame de Hennessey* (1520) was worn in most countries as a rural head-dress until the costume disappeared.

In the early sixteenth century, the "thrummed hat" of wool[1] and the straw hat were worn in most countries, and without much variation in shape. The Netherlands in particular had a coolie type, worn while working in the fields and this is seen in Breughel's pictures. The Italian countrywomen had high crowns to their rather elaborately plaited straw hats; Vecellio, at the end of the sixteenth century, gives several examples. The English market-women of 1603 (*Album Amicorum*) wore a high-crowned, narrow-brimmed example. The low or medium crown-ed straw hats were worn over the wimple-type or close-fitting type of coif; the other types were too high to take a hat.

A hat that was very popular from the early sixteenth century onwards was the thrummed wool or "Spanish felt"[2] with a medium crown and a fairly wide brim that seems to have been either floppy or stiff. Occasionally the brim was turned up at the back and pointed

1. & 2. Cunnington, *Handbook of English Costume in the 16th century*

88. FRANCE, 1529. Woman of Brittany, showing the origin of the Breton high coif. (Weiditz)

89. SPAIN, 1529. A woman of the Basque and Santander Mountains. A rare and specifically Basque headdress, with its forward bend. (Weiditz)

90. SPAIN, 1529. Basque woman. Another version of the unusual Basque headdress. (Weiditz)

91. SPAIN, 1529. Gleaning corn. The coif over the mouth is used as a protection. (Weiditz)

92. NETHERLANDS, 1529. Water carrier. The head-roll, loose sleeve and turned-up overdress are typical. (Weiditz)

93. NORTH NETHERLANDS, 1529. Mixing dough. A little-known dress from Walcheren. (Weiditz)

94. SPAIN, 1529. House dress of the Morisco woman (Weiditz)

95. FRANCE, 1529. A countrywoman of Perpignan. (Weiditz)

96. LOW COUNTRIES, 1565. Seated peasant women. (Breughel)

97. GERMANY, 1536. (Diederichs)

98. SOUTH NETHERLANDS, 1558. A working dress with typical bag. (Breughel)

99. FLANDERS, 1566. Pointed kerchief. Heavy cloth overgown. Bag and key attached to girdle. (Breughel)

52

100. ITALY, 1567. A bourgeois influence. *(Recueil de Paris)*

101. SWITZERLAND, 1564: Zürich. Bourgeois dress. The wimple-like coif, the square opening to the gown and the bands all had influence on rural dress. (Vincent)

102. SOUTH NETHERLANDS, 1568. The typical rural way of tying the apron. (Breughel)

103. SOUTH NETHERLANDS, 1568. The lirripipe-type of coif and the laced gown of elderly women. (Breughel)

104. **SPAIN**, 1580. *(Hispana Rustica)*

105. **GERMANY**, 1580, (Amman)

106. **FLANDERS**, 1580. (Amman)

107. **GERMANY**, 1580: Danzig. A young girl
without a coif. (Amman)

108. SPAIN, 1580. (Amman)

109. GERMANY, 1589: District of Nuremberg. The form of the baskets was general in many countries. (Amman)

110. GERMANY, 1580: The felt hat remains a permanent feature of rural dress. (Amman)

111. GERMANY, 1580: Nuremberg. An unmarried girl (Amman)

55

112. SWITZERLAND, c. 1580: The hooked bodice has bourgeois high sleeves. (Amman)

113. FRANCE, 1575-80: Bourges. Note the unusual sleeve of the linen shift. (Georgius Braun)

114. ITALY, 1590. The woman is old; her coif is early sixteenth century in style. The high Italian straw hat is typical. (Vecellio)

115. ITALY, 1590. Italian rural dress was elaborate. Typical corset corsage and early pattens. (Vecellio)

116. ITALY, 1590. Woman with a distaff. (Vecellio)

117. FRANCE, c. 1600. A young girl dancing. Her dress was influenced by bourgeois styles. (Montpellier Museum)

118. DENMARK, 1600. A young girl with typical Norse motif on her apron. Long plait weighted down by bell ornament. (Cornelius Kempe)

119. DENMARK, c. 1600. Typical Norse silver ornaments. (Cornelius Kempe)

downwards in front; this latter shape was popular in Great Britain until well into the nineteenth century.

Countrywomen from the fourteenth century onwards wore some kind of bag suspended from the waist. These bags were small and simple at first as in the French *Roman de la Rose* and Italian *Tacuinum Sanitatis*. In Germany and Switzerland, hanging from a strap, they were used in the fields. It was in Germany that they developed into the shape that became permanent. A Bohemian farmer's wife is illustrated as having one made of heavy material with a silver mounted top, and with it hung a knife in a sheath for use at mealtimes; together with a bunch of keys they form a sort of reticule, an imitation of the more elaborate objects worn by wealthier women. In the early seventeenth century Danish Faroe Island women had bags and knives.

The material and silver-mounted bag, without its curious "pouches", passed into the northern Netherlands where it is still used today with the Zeeland costume, though the sheathed knife, keys, scissors and watch, also worn in the late eighteenth century, have vanished. I have not found any signs of any kind of bag or its appendages being worn by Spanish or English countrywomen.

Seventeenth century

The seventeenth century was a transitional period for rural peoples and their costume. The peasant workers were now theoretically free in western Europe, though in some countries they were more or less bound to the landowner's estate. Most of the countries were plunged in lengthy and devastating wars, a fact very often reflected in the costume of the poorer people, especially in the latter half of the century. The northern Netherlands, Switzerland and England were the exceptions.

This century is also the most difficult for visual information. The artists and even the engravers were principally interested in portraying court people and high dignataries and in discovering the possibilities of classical landscape; even the Italians dress their "Adoring Shepherds" of this period in near-classical garments. Holland is an exception to this rule; and luckily there are also artists like Velasquez and Murillo in Spain and the Le Nains and de la Tour in France who were also interested in rural life, and who also show through their costume paintings the poverty and difficulty of peasant life at this period.

In England there is extremely little data for this period, but luckily the great engraver and traveller Hollar has given us engravings of rural women in nearly every country of western Europe, and his careful recording of detail is of immense value. For instance, his engraving of a woman of *Matriciana* in the Abruzzi links with the Vecellio engraving of the same district in the previous century, and this dress can be traced almost unaltered until the early twentieth century.

Hollar also gives engravings of examples of individual town costume; this fashion probably started in the sixteenth century and developed to a large extent in France, the Netherlands, Germany, Switzerland and Italy; it is apt to be confused with the rural regional dresses – actually it was from this developing town costume that the rural peasants took their fashion. It was usually stiffer and more elaborate than the rural costume, but not so exaggerated as that of the noblewomen, especially those attached to the local courts, large or small. England, never having had independent self-governing towns, did not develop this individual town fashion.

During the seventeenth century the true regional dress does not develop much, but there came to be a marked difference in rural costume from one country to another, a deviation which increased as each country ceased to be ruled by a small number of great feudal landowners and began to develop national characteristics of its own. The German costume particularly developed a certain stiffness and square effect, which became more marked in the following centuries, whereas the French dress showed, with a few exceptions, a tendency to a graceful, easy and rather simple line, which from this period onwards was characteristic of that country.

At the beginning of the seventeenth century the corset-bodice was still very square and mostly sleeveless in the southern countries, but generally with rather tight sleeves in the Netherlands, Germany and England. Quite a few countries had a back lacing to their corset, and the full chemisette with sleeves was often worn under the corset. In France it was mostly tight fitting with an upright open collar, copying the ladies of fashion. The chemisette or smock had a front opening and fairly long wide sleeves.

The kerchief was much worn with a point at the back and weighted with little crochet bobbles, and this fashion remained with the French and many costumes of other countries. In Italy the chemisette was worn fuller and was usually trimmed with a frilled edge; but occasionally the falling ruff was worn and the sleeves were very full.

In the first half of the seventeenth century the laced corset-bodice was very much in evidence, often with sleeves. The front retained its sixteenth-century shape, also the rather large falling ruff; this also applies to the German corset-bodice.

The Dutch-Danish Amager dress retained the ruff, but with a closed bodice and three-quarter length sleeve with an undersleeve. This type of sleeve features in the Dutch costume. The Scandinavian

120. ITALY, 1642. The Abruzzi dress remained practically unaltered until the twentieth century. (Hollar)

121. DENMARK, 1612: Sildea. White turban. Red yoke to pinkish red gown. Blue centre under petticoat. White belt. Yellow sleeves and stockings. (Georgius Braun, *Civitates Orbis Terrarum*)

122. NORTH NETHERLANDS, *c.* 1631. (Rembrandt)

123. NORTH NETHERLANDS, 1657: Zeeland. Farm worker. (From a rare drawing of a working dress and 'cover' apron Nic. Visser, Zeeuws Museum, Middelburg)

dress had a flat, large cape-like collar. In England, as far as can be ascertained, the bodice in the early seventeenth century was similar to that of the sixteenth century – tight-fitting narrow sleeves, the sleeve-roll being retained, a loose front and a small ruff.

By the second half of the seventeenth century the tight-fitting laced corset-bodice is less in evidence, though in the northern Dutch provinces and in Flanders it was still generally worn. It is seen in the etchings of Rembrandt and the pictures of Jan Victoors. A fur edging to the corset which formed a V at the back gives what is known as the *Noord Holland* dress a regional appearance.

As the seventeenth century progressed, in the Netherlands the looser basqued bodice, which was still low cut but now had low set and fuller sleeves under bourgeois influence, was the more generally worn and became the basic *jak* or jacket of the Dutch costume, together with the sixteenth-century partlet or *placard* which filled in the gap back and front, and was partially covered by a folded kerchief. The main variations were the sleeves and the basque which followed the fashion of the day.

This same bodice with basque or lappets and with full sleeves was worn in France, England and Spain, but not very much in Germany and apparently not at all in Italy.

The French countrywomen at this period wore a square bodice, mostly fastened by hooks in front; also a loose jacket, hip length, with long or three-quarter length, rather full, sleeves. The chemisette or smock was very much in evidence with both the sleeveless bodice and the jacket. It had both a wide, turn-down collar with points and a smaller turned-over collar, but the kerchief was still worn, tucked into the bodice in front. This fashion was still in vogue in the nineteenth century. The smock and collar were of light-coloured linen. This type of smock and collar was probably also worn in the late seventeenth century in the Scandinavian countries, as it appears in the eighteenth-century dresses.

In England and Germany the wide kerchief was often replaced by a square, deep linen collar over the bodice.

By the second half of the seventeenth century the basic line of the corset-bodice and the basqued bodice, except for small details, remained unaltered.

As the peasants began to own their own plots of land and the women to work in them, the skirts became shorter and fuller, especially in Germany and the Scandinavian countries, and probably also in Switzerland. On the edges of the skirt were bands of material; this was a borrowed bourgeois fashion which had long been discarded by the fashionable but remained a permanency where rural costume was con-

124. GERMANY, seventeenth century. A much-laden woman, with house keys and bread knife. (Diederichs)

125. NETHERLANDS, 1657: Walcheren. Woman in farmyard with (plastron) hooked bodice. Apron, skirt. All almost unaltered to the present day. (Hofje van Wou Grypskerk, Zeeuws Museum, Middelburg)

126. NETHERLANDS, 1700: Zaandam. A bourgeois style that had strong influence on rural dress. (From a photograph)

127. GERMANY, mid-seventeenth century. A working dress. Straw hat and loose sleeve. (Diederichs)

cerned. The skirts were of heavy material and so were the underskirts, as drawers were not worn.

Striped skirts, so much worn in the next century, began to appear. There is a German drawing of a haymaker in an underskirt of light material, with a rolled up apron or top skirt which extends from waist to hips. This rolled-up garment is also illustrated in Hollar's engraving of a Swedish costume. The apron is fuller than in the sixteenth century, mostly made of coloured or white coarse linen, but red or black cloth aprons were also worn; they still did not extend to the back of the wearer. Working aprons were of hempen cloth. In Flanders and probably other countries they were more scanty, tighter, pulled round the waist to the back and meeting with two points – an old model. For special occasions, especially in the northern countries, the aprons were tightly pleated or folded in wide pleats, as they still are in Marken.

The cloak is not usually illustrated in the seventeenth century, probably because a jacket was often worn over the bodice, but obviously it was still worn in winter and on journeys. In Germany it was long and full and fastened at the neck. In Denmark at this period a cloak was worn over the head and was given by fathers to their daughters on marriage.

The bourgeois *huik*, that curious full mantle of Moorish origin, was the winter garment of the upper and middle classes of Spain, the Netherlands and southern Germany in the seventeenth century. It eventually became the *falie* or *pleureuse*, the mourning cloak of the people of Flanders and several other countries.

Shoes were square-toed, mostly with front flap, and in Germany they came high over the ankle and were tied with a leather thong. Soles were thicker and were of wood or cork, and for special occasions rosettes or bows appeared on the front of the shoe.

There is a Hollar etching of a Dutch countrywoman with wooden sandals with leather straps. Wooden shoes were used when scrubbing in the same way as they are today. In the Hollar etching of an English countrywoman she is wearing wooden pattens mounted on an iron ring.

The coifs of this period developed the lines which they retained during the following centuries, but the regional differences were not yet very apparent, nor the exaggerations which developed at the end of the eighteenth century. Nevertheless, although there were many similarities from country to country, certain countries and certain regions of those countries were creating their own distinctive head-dress.

The fourteenth-century loose, long hood-like kerchief with pointed ends was worn by the peasant women painted by Velasquez and Murillo, and in a 1623 *Album Amicorum*[1] miniature the Spanish

1. British Museum MSS

128. NORTH NETHERLANDS, *c.* 1700. This style is almost identical with the present Volendam coif. She carries her kerchief with crocheted '*Akkertjes*'. (P. van den Berge)

129. DANISH, 1739: Jutland. (Ellen Andersen)

130. DENMARK, 1758: Amager (Dutch-Danish). The Amager dress came from the North

131. ITALY, eighteenth century. Typical pointed kerchief and loose sleeves usually tied by ribbons in Italy. (Tiepolo)

countrywoman wears a heavy cloth mantilla-like head covering reaching to the shoulders, similar to those worn by nineteenth-century Sardinian women.

De la Tour in his early seventeenth-century French painting shows the *bongrace* type of coif, and Georgius Braun in 1612[1] illustrates the "floating" coif – flat on top with a deep frill to the shoulder and hanging down at the back; this shape was adopted by many countries – France, the greater part of the northern and southern Netherlands and the southern part of Germany. This coif does not seem to have been worn in England. The shape there and in many other countries was oval, framing the face, drawn in at the back with a short protruding frill. This simple type of coif either with a frill of varying length or with wings covering the cheeks or turned back from them, survived even after the rest of the costume had disappeared.

In the northern Dutch provinces women wore a round head-dress with a fairly high round crown gathered into a button, trimmed with a band or bands of ribbon round the base. This coif was regional to this district, and survives in the Marken head-dress of today. Rembrandt in his etchings and Jan Victoors in his paintings show this type of head-dress. Scandinavia and Dutch Friesland had a high helmet-like coif, which was also worn in Germany and Denmark. Norwegian women wore a rather high cylindrical shaped coif of birch, whalebone or thin wood over which were stretched several pieces of coloured material sewn together. In Denmark the *crespigne* ring or band which keeps the hair in place dates from prehistoric times, as does the band in early Norwegian head-dress. This type of head-dress, beflowered and decorated in various ways, was adopted as a bridal crown by the girls of the Scandinavian countries, Germany and Switzerland well into the nineteenth century.

Hats were still worn over the coifs. The steeple-crowned hat with a wide brim was worn in England, Germany and Flanders, and a medium-crowned straw hat with a soft and shady brim, probably a summer working hat, is often seen in Dutch, Flemish and German pictures, but it was not generally worn until the eighteenth century. Hats were, naturally, not worn when milk or water jugs were carried balanced on a round stuffed pad on the head.

The fifteenth-century thrummed or felt hat with medium crown and upturned brim was still worn in the Netherlands and Germany as part of the winter clothing.

Sheathed knives and various types of bags were still worn hanging from the waist in the Netherlands, and especially in Germany, with the addition in the latter country of the household keys.

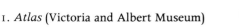
1. *Atlas* (Victoria and Albert Museum)

132. ITALY, 1796. Peasant girl. (Bicci)

133. SPAIN, 1799, The rural felt hat was very general in western Europe. *(Colección General de Los Trages de España, 1799)*

134. NORWAY, eighteenth century: Osterfjord. (Lexow)

135. NORWAY, eighteenth century. (Lexow)

136. NETHERLANDS, 1790: Friesland. Noblewoman in gala dress holding sun hat. (F. W. S. van Thienen and J. D. Duyvetter, *Klederdrachten*)

Eighteenth century onward

By the eighteenth century the basic garments – i.e. corset-bodice, jacket skirt, apron and coif – had become more or less static in design, though the details varied according to the degree of influence exercised by bourgeois fashion.

In the beginning of the century the northern countries – Scandinavia, North Holland, northern Germany and the German part of Switzerland, as well as the mountainous regions of Italy in the south – retained many of the sixteenth- even the fifteenth-century details, such as the small ruff, a square, flat, and edged yoke, following the same line as the fifteenth-century *placard* (frontal piece) and the Phrygian-Saxon cap. Countries not so frequented by travellers, and not affected by the gradual increase of industrialisation, retained these influences well into the nineteenth century. The more contact country people had with towns, travellers and industry, the more the rural costume was influenced by seasonal fashions, though many years after town and society women had discarded them.

Although there had been for some time a few distinctive regional dresses, or features, such as the head-dresses of the Basques, the costume of the North Holland people and their cousins, the Amager folk of Denmark, and the inhabitants of the Abruzzi mountains, the costumes which could be assigned to one particular village or religion or status did not blossom into their full glory before the middle or even the last quarter of the eighteenth century. Only then were the better-off peasants in a position to indulge in "infinite variety" and richness of design and materials, though this was mostly apparent in the gala dresses for Sundays and feast days.

Complete freedom from tied service to landlords, the buying of their own farms, and the abolition of the sumptuary laws were, as we have seen, the causes of these changes; the people were then left to buy as their pockets, taste and village fashion dictated. When a costume was regional, *what* you might wear and *how* you might wear your dress and its details was more or less rigid. Nevertheless, new details were introduced by young men and girls – probably, as in Zeeland, up to 1940 at a local feast, when the new details would appear. But the basic garments remained unchanged.

In the eighteenth and nineteenth centuries the following garments prevailed. The sixteenth-century type corset-bodice was still worn, especially in Italy where the wide and laced opening predominated, and also in Switzerland where the shape was unchanged and was completed by the original partlet, deep falling ruff and cut-away jacket with upper- and undersleeves (double sleeves) seen in much earlier illustrations.

137. FRANCE, eighteenth century: The roll is always worn when carrying objects on the head. Footwear is wooden sabots. (St. Sauveur)

138. NORTH NETHERLANDS, 1780: District of Zaandam. Rich bourgeois in the traditional 'Kaper'. (F. W. S. van Thienen and J. Duyvetter, *Klederdrachten*)

139. NORTH NETHERLANDS, 1811: Walcheren. Villager going to market. Straw hat over linen coif. Flowered chintz corsage. Brocade skirt with checked cotton apron. (Maaskamp)

140. NORTH NETHERLANDS, 1811: Friesland. Country girl selling butter. (Maaskamp)

For summer, a short full-sleeved blouse or chemisette was worn under the corset and the kerchief was tucked into the corset. Towards the middle of the nineteenth century the kerchief became more like the eighteenth-century ladies' *fichu,* and was worn mostly with the distinctive town costume so general in Switzerland.

In France the hooked bodice, with a long basque, was very much influenced by bourgeois fashion. The bodice generally had three-quarter length sleeves, and was worn with a chemisette with a turned-back collar and sleeves which often came below those of the hooked bodice. Over this garment a kerchief with a deep back point was frequently worn. The general effect was loose and easy, and though the laced corset-bodice was still used, it had not the stiffness of the German and Swiss models.

This easy effect is also apparent in the dress of the southern provinces of the Netherlands. In Flanders and in England the hooked bodice was much influenced by contemporary fashion and became very high-waisted, though still with basque; but it was always separate from the skirt.

This separation of bodice and skirt after the late fourteenth or early fifteenth centuries is very characteristic of rural dress. The reason for the separation was that the corset-bodice or hooked bodice could be discarded and the wearer could work in smock and skirt in southern countries, or in the wide back and front partlet over the smock or a sort of under-bodice, as is till done in the Dutch province of Zeeland.

The Breton bodice, which is really a sort of short jacket, had in a few cases a very unusual cut. The breast line ended in a curve rather like a new moon lying on its back; this line was repeated three times, giving the impression of three garments.. The only other garment I have noted of this type, but with a single curve, was worn by Norwegian and Sardinian peasants of the same period; contrary to all other rural dresses it seems to have no logical derivation. The men's jackets had much the same line. The northern provinces of the Netherlands retained the square-cut bodice, which had a rigid effect, especially in the more remote villages, and it was covered by a crossed-over kerchief. In places more exposed to fashionable influence this rigid look gave way at the end of the eighteenth century to the long basqued bodice, and in the beginning of the nineteenth century it acquired an Empire look.

The bodice tended to develop regional details, but on the whole the square rigid look of an earlier period was retained in remote villages, while in places nearer the towns the influence of the late eighteenth-century and early nineteenth-century fashions became apparent. This influence is particularly noticeable in the dress of the southern provinces of the Netherlands which followed the lines of the French cos-

141. SWITZERLAND, 1815: Guggisberg. Grey
jacket, red bodice, dark grey skirt, blue apron,
white socks, red tongue on shoe.

142. SWITZERLAND, 1815. Haymaker from the
Tessin. (Josy) (Koenig)

143. SWITZERLAND, 1815: Fribourg. A town dress
which has an influence on rural dress. The hat is
rare, but a similar one is part of a town dress in
Friesland, North Netherlands. (Josy)

144. ITALY, 1814. (Pinelli)

145. NETHERLANDS, 1825: Zeeland. The only
Zeeland dress that has the rigid *stiklief* corset-
corsage in plain black velvet or flowered brocade.
(Zeeuws Museum, Middelburg)

146. ITALY, 1826. *Bongrace* coif, embroidered
apron, loose sleeves, mittens. Frascati

147. SWEDEN, 1827: Elfdal (Forssell)

148. SWEDEN, 1827: Torna Harad. (Forssell)

tumes, whereas dress in the northern provinces had a Scandinavian look. This difference remained, and still exists.

In the late eighteenth and early nineteenth centuries the Scandinavian bodice continued rigid in line, but, as in Switzerland, varied a great deal in detail. It had a short rather than long basque and, when not hooked, the front opening was filled in by the partlet – a fashion which became very general in Norway in the nineteenth century and was what might be called a national characteristic.

The Danish-Dutch Amager dress remained very traditional, but adopted a brightly coloured handkerchief imported from Barcelona, which was worn rather high on the breast and close round the neck.

The Danish dress disappeared after 1850.

German and Austrian countrywomen retained the rigid, laced corset-bodice, sometimes with a bolero-like effect with long, rather tight sleeves; sometimes the *Mieder,* as it was called, was sleeveless. A kerchief was worn tucked into the corset-bodice, or, when worn outside, into the waist of the skirt. The German costume was definitely very regional, basically sixteenth-century, but in some parts – particularly in southern Germany – more influenced by the eighteenth century, and this influence persisted until the dress disappeared.

In Spain both the hooked and laced bodice was worn. As usual, when hooked, the sleeves were long and tight, and when laced the chemisette or smock had full short sleeves as in France and Italy. The kerchief was usually worn over the bodice and of floral design, sometimes fringed and often tied behind.

In England the bodice was purely eighteenth century, with a wide kerchief mostly falling in points in front and deep at the back. Only the Welsh bodice, or bed gown, as it was called, with its very long basque, had a European look with certain regional details.

In all countries in the first quarter of the eighteenth century fashions were influenced by those of the previous century, but gradually, as more manufactured materials became available and were more widely distributed, the rural skirt became fuller and more varied materials were used. The wide fashionable panniers were rarely worn, though a pannier-like effect was obtained by looping up the skirt; this was particularly noticeable in Auvergne, where attractive linings were shown, and English countrywomen also occasionally adopted this fashion.

The fashionable hoop was an impossible article of clothing for the countrywoman, but the same effect was obtained by the use of many petticoats and also by a stuffed roll tied round the waist; this was still used by Dutch peasants in the early twentieth century. As the skirts became somewhat shorter the general look was rococo.

Bands on the edge of the skirt were used in Spain, Italy, Switzerland and the Scandinavian countries, and occasionally in France and Germany. In England the skirt had no particular rural character, but in Wales in the early nineteenth century a striped material was much used; also in France, the Netherlands and Belgium.

There is very little variation in the line of the skirts in the nineteenth century, but in the use of material, colour and decoration they were definitely regional.

In Italy the material used for gala occasions was usually a heavy cloth, elaborately embroidered or trimmed with lace, bands and braid. In the Netherlands, though very gay colours and beautifully patterned cotton damasks were worn in the late eighteenth and early nineteenth centuries, they were never trimmed or banded, though they were edged with a braid as a protection against wear, as were the Welsh skirts.

In the last quarter of the nineteenth century and in the twentieth century a good deal of black was used – the result of the rather sombre clothes of the bourgeois women of the late nineteenth century.

Skirts in Germany and Switzerland were often very short, even for that period, especially in the mountainous districts. In Switzerland they were in coloured stripes, but, even in the early nineteenth century, black material was also used, and was sometimes, as in the Scandinavian countries, closely pleated. Black was not much used in Norway, but a good deal of dark blue, brown and red, mostly edged with braid and often fairly short.

In France many beautiful materials were used for gala wear. Skirts and bodices were often of the same material. Many petticoats continued to be worn by rural people until the costume disappeared, and this custom, together with the rather heavy short skirt, marked the big gap that existed and increased between rural and bourgeois dress as the nineteenth century advanced. This trend continued until the rural dress was clearly something different and apart from the general appearance of the mass of men and women. Even when a bourgeois dress was adopted (plus a rural coif and apron, as it was between 1870 and 1880) it remained true to the fashion of those years until the time when all vestige of regional dress disappeared.

By the middle of the eighteenth century it was the apron that underwent the biggest transformation. Except in sixteenth-century Italy, especially the Abruzzi district, aprons had always been simple garments, occasionally "honeycombed" at the waist, usually white or natural colour, of fine or coarse linen or hemp, though heavy dark materials, especially black, were used.

With the freeing of rural costume from the sumptuary laws regarding

149. NORTH NETHERLANDS, *c.* 1860: Walcheren. Straw hat lined blue, with blue or mauve ribbons. Coloured printed cotton or woven silk and cotton-mixture bodice. (Composite drawing from photographs)

150. DENMARK, early nineteenth century: From Odense. (Ellen Andersen)

151. DENMARK, eighteenth to nineteenth century: Amager. An indication of mourning. (Andersen)

152. DENMARK, early nineteenth century bride's dress. (Dansk National Museum)

153. DENMARK, 1848. A Dutch-Danish dress with the addition of flowered silk kerchief imported from Barcelona. The style dates from the early seventeenth century. (Dansk National Museum)

materials, and with the invention of the printed chintzes and striped cottons and calicoes, the apron, anyhow for Sundays and gala days, became a gay and festive garment. White for aprons was much less common, though it was used by Norwegian women and by the "White Bride of Marken". In England, however, the big white apron was worn by countrywomen until the early twentieth century. The Italians used their skill with the needle on their aprons; lovely woven materials were also worn as well as heavy cloth trimmed with coloured braid. The eighteenth and nineteenth century Italian apron seems to have been a question of personal taste rather than regional fashion. The workaday apron, especially in the mountains, was naturally simple and made of washable materials.

Aprons in Norway were now often white. Embroidery and "banding" was used on them, but on the whole elaborate patterning seems to have been kept for the bodice and sometimes the skirt. In Telemark the aprons were black and in Niemendal coloured.

The Dutch-Danish Amager aprons were pale blue for daily wear, black, red or white for church, folded into pleats like those of Marken today. Two aprons were worn by married women for christenings, and in 1830-40 boys wore blue pleated aprons.

In eighteenth-century Switzerland the aprons were often black or brown and of heavy woollen material. In the nineteenth century, especially towards the middle of the century, striped cotton aprons became fashionable; the type of stripe seems to have been regional, broad in some places, narrow in others. Switzerland had a flourishing cotton printing industry starting in the early nineteenth century. Koenig[1] writes of the Hallau dress that when the corset-bodice and skirt were black, the apron was black, and when the skirt was striped the apron was striped. Coloured silk aprons were also worn in the nineteenth century, especially with the costumes influenced by the town.

The aprons of eighteenth- and nineteenth-century Germany differed from those in France, the Netherlands and Switzerland, in that the gay, checked, striped and flowered cotton aprons so popular in those countries do not seem to have been used. The working apron in the beginning of the eighteenth century seems to have been white, as it was in the seventeenth century. Later it became brown, black or blue. For Sundays black pleated silk seems to have been popular in some regions, though blue was often worn. There was a good deal of bourgeois influence in the wearing of black silk aprons.

The Dutch apron also became very gay in the eighteenth century; it was made of flowered cotton or chintz materials manufactured in Amsterdam. Coloured aprons continued into the early part of the next

1. Early nineteenth century

154. GERMANY, nineteenth century: From the
Ochsenfurt district, Bavaria. (Baur-Heinhold.
Deutsche Trachten)

155. NORWAY, 1870: Setesdaal. This dress is of
very ancient and primitive origin. (From a
photograph)

156. GERMANY, nineteenth century: Schwalmen.
Gala dress. Some German and Swiss skirts were
shorter than most rural skirts. The curious little
'pill box' type hat was also worn in Switzerland.
(Helm)

157. GERMANY, nineteenth century: Schwalmen.
(Helm)

century, but in the middle period black aprons of silk merino and other fancy but heavy materials were worn on Sundays and striped blue or grey aprons were worn for working in. The use of a Sunday and a workday apron continued in Zeeland, though the everyday apron is now of black and white woven material.

In the northern parts of the country a gay, practical apron was devised. The upper part was of checked and colourful cotton, the lower part of plain blue, black or red. The upper part usually wore out first and could be easily renewed.

In France aprons varied greatly from region to region, though a good deal of white linen was used in the eighteenth century, when the skirts were striped. In Burgundy beautiful and richly bordered silk was worn for special occasions, and in the late nineteenth century the Bretons had lovely embroidered silk aprons, though the older women wore black. Rather narrow striped aprons were worn in Provence.

In Spain the aprons, anyhow for gala occasions, were gay and flowered and not striped or checked.

An embroidered short affair with a braided under-apron was worn in Ibiza in the Balearic Islands, rather Italian in look. Today a short apron of woven silk material is still worn.

In England in the eighteenth century the aprons were mostly white, and so continued until the end of the next century and up to 1910. They were very voluminous and were made of heavy cotton. In Wales where a distinct regional dress developed at the end of the eighteenth century, a small checked Welsh cotton in soft colours was used for most aprons, though white ones were also worn.

The cloak, cape and its relation the shawl, survived into the nine-teenth century; the shawl into the twentieth. When worn the cloak kept its long, full seventeenth-century shape. It varied little from the hooded garment worn by most women of all classes as an outdoor garment, only the hoods of the rural people were smaller, because they had only to cover the normal size coif or head-dress of the eighteenth and early nineteenth centuries and not the vast hair arrangements and headgear of fashionable women. The cloak is a difficult garment to trace in this period. Illustrators of numerous books who delighted in the details of the many gay dresses were not interested in the rather dull garment that covered the finery. Nevertheless, cloaks were certainly worn and are often referred to. As the cloak was an old and very traditional garment it probably changed little in shape or material. As a chapter of this book is devoted solely to the mantle, a few general notes will suffice here.

In Spain the ancient *huik* head-covering and mantle of the ladies shortened itself to a shoulder length head-dress and might be called

158. SARDINIA, nineteenth century. Gala dress.
   The skirt is of scarlet cloth and the embroidered
   border and head-dress white. (After a
   photograph)

159. SARDINIA, nineteenth century. The wimple-
   type coif is interesting, also the Spanish-type
   head-dress. (Emma Calderini)

160. ITALY, twentieth century: Calabria. The
   skirts are usually scarlet cloth showing white
   underskirt, bodice and apron in a dark colour and
   the curious and very individual back flounce
   in bright colours. (From a photograph)

161. ITALY, twentieth century: Potenza, Lucania.
   this dress is in daily use and shows the *bongrace* headdress, low corset-corsage apron and
   banded pleated skirt, all surviving from an
   earlier period. (From a photograph)

national rather than regional. It was worn in Spain until the nineteenth century and was also and still is a part of one of the many forms of Sardinian head-dress.

In Italy wide silk scarves or shawls were mostly worn, but the countrywomen round Genoa wore the *calecos,* a beautifully printed and patterned calico head-covering which hung down to the feet: this was used for Sundays and fêtes.

In Portugal the fish-sellers of Agueda still wear a black head mantle topped with traditional cushion to support the fish basket. This mantle much resembles those worn by ladies in sixteenth-century Moorish Spain.

In France, the cloak was apparently of light materials, often flowered prints, and not so heavy or ample as in some other countries – though in the nineteenth century it became plain in colour, long and bourgeois.

In Germany, on the Island of Sylt, a queer square mantle was used for covering the whole head, with a small opening for the face, and descending to the hips. In Switzerland a black cloak covering the face was worn in Fribourg, the only one to be recorded by Koenig, that excellent writer on late eighteenth- and early nineteenth-century Swiss costume.

In Belgium the cloaks in what survived of the dress were long, black and hooded and much influenced by bourgeois fashion.

In Flanders in 1930 there was a survival of the ancient Moorish Spanish mantilla or *huik,* known as the *falie* or *pleureuse,* a black, long mantle covering the head and most of the face, and worn for funerals.

In the southern part of the Netherlands, the hooded cloak, the ancient *falie,* was worn well into the twentieth century, and is still worn by a very few old and well-to-do farmers' wives in the province of Zeeland, Flanders, much the same type as in early nineteenth-century prints of Ostend. A short, rather more colourful cape for spring and autumn was worn in Zeeland and when that disappeared its place was taken by a plush shawl which is still worn. In winter the Scheveningen fishwives still wear a heavy lined cloak, but in the more northern parts of the country heavy jackets or jacket coats and not cloaks were worn in the nineteenth century.

In England the hooded cloak, in black or red, was very popular, as it was also in Wales, though there the hood was bigger to cover the high hat, and purple was also used. The red cloak in England might be called the one national rural garment.

In Skye in the early nineteenth century, contemporary drawings show a very old woman wearing a three-quarter length mantle without hood, and an eighteenth-century Highland woman wearing a shaggy mantle with high collar much resembling the garment of the sixteenth-century "wild Irish".

162. SARDINIA, 1898. Tightly pleated skirt much worn in Sardinia. The apron has a Greek rural influence. (Fonni, *Costume di Gala*)

163. U.S.A., nineteenth century: Pennsylvania Dutch (German). The basic north-west rural garments are present in this Amish dress still in daily use. The pointed kerchief can be seen as early as the sixteenth century in France, in North Netherlands in the seventeenth century, and from then onwards in most western countries. (From a photograph)

Irishwomen wore a three-quarter length cloak with the top part forming a hood of traditional design, and today a lovely cloak is worn in Kinsale.

Shoes in the eighteenth century, though naturally heavier and stronger than those worn by town people, show a definite fashionable influence, especially those for Sundays and fête days. During the eighteenth century, the wooden shoe, sabot, *klomp* or clog and the ancient patten kept their traditional use as a protection for the leather shoe against wet and mud.

The Netherlands at the beginning of the eighteenth century had a soft leather shoe with ties, also the backless shoe with a wooden sole, patten-shape. Later a lower type of leather shoe with more pointed toes and trimmed with silver buckles came into fashion and this lasted well into the nineteenth century when the modern leather laced shoe was adopted. In isolated villages, like Staphorst, the silver-buckled shoe is still worn for Sundays. *Klompen,* the Dutch wooden shoes, were always used for land work and outside scrubbing and rough work, but were never brought into the house.

In Belgium shoes followed the same pattern, though the buckled shoe seemed to be less worn, and where regional dress survived sabots were used.

In the Meuse district gaiters were worn over leather shoes. In the Ardennes the *galoche,* leather shoes with wooden soles and heels and straps fastened over the instep, were worn, but not sabots.

The Dutch Amager people of Denmark wore simple silver or steel square buckles on their shoes until the costume disappeared in the 1870's.

Other Scandinavian countrywomen also had silver- or steel- buckled shoes, tied slippers and, in the northern part of Norway, a strong high shoe made from skins. The wooden shoe did not seem to be much worn in the Scandinavian countries.

In Switzerland the buckled shoe and the leather one with a turned back flap were equal favourites. The flap was often red with dagged edges; this type of shoe seems peculiar to Switzerland, where wooden-soled sandals were also worn, but not wooden shoes.

In Germany a rather shapeless leather shoe was worn by country-women. It was square-toed, low-heeled, often rather high at the ankles and tied with a bow. Rosettes were frequently used. Silver buckles do not seem to have been much worn, except in a few regions, for instance in Ulm, where the dress was very traditional and colourful. Wooden shoes were worn, but not so generally as in the Netherlands, Belgium and France.

In France the shoes for Sundays and fêtes varied according to the region and were inclined to follow the town fashion – the pointed leather slipper tied with a bow and with buckles and in some districts laced, were worn in the early nineteenth century. The sabots were universal, as the women worked a great deal on the land.

In the mountainous districts of Spain the *espadrille* or laced sandal was considered the most practical footwear. Spain also had the eighteenth-century buckled shoe, but a laced sandal like the *espadrille* was used.

In England, Wales and Ireland a short leather shoe, mostly tied, was worn. These shoes had rather square toes and thick soles and were occasionally adorned with buckles. Wooden shoes of the hollowed-out sabot type were never worn, but the solid wooden patten raised on iron runners was in constant use by countrywomen. This type of patten seems to have been especially English, as Peter Kalm, the Swedish traveller, in 1745 remarked that "the English farmer's wife thrusts her leather or stuff shoes into the wooden patten with its iron ring."

Stockings in the eighteenth and nineteenth centuries were all knitted and even when worn with gay and elaborate dresses were of heavy make, in contrast to the light cotton and silk of the townswoman. Only in Italy, France and Switzerland, if the rural women lived on the outskirts of a town, were the stockings lighter in colour and texture.

Mostly dark colours were worn, but butcher blue and red were worn in the Netherlands, Switzerland and Norway, and white in France and Switzerland.

German stockings were usually blue or white; the white knitted, and patterned. The Austrians wore white. It is interesting to note that, with their early nineteenth-century dress the fishwives of Fisherrow near Edinburgh now wear nylon for everyday and silk for gala occasions.

The head-dresses and coifs from the middle of the eighteenth century for at least a hundred years multiplied both in shape, size and regional importance. In the years 1749-60 a dainty coif was adopted by all classes in most western European countries and this fashion lasted for some considerable time, and was renewed in the middle of the nineteenth century, when married women of a certain age wore an elaborate coif. A smaller version was worn right up to 1914. It is possible that the fashionable eighteenth-century coif was influenced by Marie Antoinette's interest in rustic pleasures and also the interest aroused by the writings of Jean-Jacques Rousseau. Certainly the adoption of the flat straw hat, which had been worn by country folk since Greek times, was a rural usage copied by fashionable ladies. The reverse of this was the nineteenth-century ladies' befrilled and beribboned coif and the fashionable straw poke-bonnet, which definitely had its effect on the regional costume of particular districts in various countries. The difference between the fashionable and rural cap or coif was that the ladies wore theirs indoors and the rural women all the time.

In the end the wearing of the coif was a distinguishing mark of a farming community. As the nineteenth century advanced and the dresses worn were the same as the townswomen's the coif was the only regional garment retained apart from the apron which was far less regionally variable.

In western Europe in the early eighteenth century the coif did not change much in shape, but by the middle of the century the virtual disappearance of the sumptuary laws and the increasing prosperity of the farming communities had a marked influence on the development of regional costume, particularly the headgear.

As the last hundred years of regional costume is fairly well-documented and above all well-illustrated, I will not give detailed descriptions, nor the numerous regional names by which similar types of coifs were known, but I will endeavour to indicate the basic lines that survived from the past.

It is not easy to say why a particular country adopted its style of head-dress, but there are a few generalisations possible. For instance, France and Switzerland were makers of lace and fine net, and they used a great deal of both for their coifs; this especially applies to French Switzerland.

Holland also used a good deal of lace on their Sunday coifs, but this was mostly imported from Belgium and northern France.

Belgium rapidly adopted bourgeois dress; only a very few districts had a regional dress and then not a very elaborate one.

The southern German coifs were akin to their neighbour's, the French Alsace in particular retained the "floating" coif, so much worn in France. The northern part of Germany had a close-fitting coif, often of coloured material, which could be covered by a hat or shawl in bad weather.

Italian women did not wear their lace for head-dress, but, curiously enough, folded heavy linen or cloth, keeping nearly always to the early sixteenth-century *bongrace* line. This was probably a good protection against the sun, and water-jars could be carried easily on the flattened top.

The Spanish mostly wore as head-dress the long shoulder-length kerchief, sometimes loose, as in the early seventeenth century, sometimes tied under the chin.

Scandinavian women wore more coloured material coifs than linen ones, and the high Phrygian type was still predominant.

In the British Isles, with the exception of Wales, certain Yorkshire districts and the fishing villages, Newhaven, Musselburgh and Fish-errow near Edinburgh, regional coifs never developed. When what might be called a "country cap" ceased to be worn in the first half of the nineteenth century the sun-bonnet took its place and was retained in Worcestershire and Herefordshire until 1914; this was only worn outdoors. It was, however, a specifically English head-dress.

The following are some of the individual types of coifs in various countries.

France had a great variety of coifs and an even greater variety of names for them. In the province of Brittany alone there were at least 24 different names, 14 in Breton and 10 in French, amongst them *henin*. This cylindrical or barrel-shaped coif was worn in Brittany in the sixteenth century and is still worn in the province for Pardons and special occasions. Though there is far more variety than formerly, they all have a built-up look, rather like a Bishop's mitre. This is a characteristic found also in a coif from Saloros outside Lisbon and from district in French Switzerland. In the nineteenth century the *henin* type of coif was placed on the back of the head with the hair fashionably arranged in front, whereas in the early eighteenth century the hair was always hidden. Though some of the French coifs tend to be high and stiffened, the majority had a soft, full crown, with a long or short floating frill, according to the region, and in the eighteenth and nineteenth centuries, apart from Brittany and parts of Normandy, they were always graceful, as was the rest of the costume.

Throughout the eighteenth and nineteenth centuries the flat straw hat was worn, particularly in the southern part of the country.

The Italian eighteenth- and nineteenth-century head-dress remained very traditional and did not vary so much in shape as in some other countries. It consisted mostly of the *bongrace*-type coif and the fourteenth-century kerchief with the long front ends, very similar to those worn by Velasquez's peasant figures. This type of head-covering is still worn in Italy and Spain, but the kerchief is now tied under the chin. The *bongrace*, still flat on the crown of the head with back hanging ends, was of plain linen which was also embroidered and was worn until 1922. Another and rarer headgear was a small coif of net fastened with a dagger-like pin which appeared in a Stradanus print of the early seventeenth century. It seems to have been confined to one region.

There were many head-dresses in Sardinia until quite lately, but the principal one was the pointed hanging kerchief reaching to the shoulders, of fairly heavy material, often bordered and identical with that of the Spanish countrywoman of 1623[1].

Spain mostly used this type of kerchief either hanging loose or tied under the chin.

1. British Museum, *Album Amicorum*

In Germany in the last half of the eighteenth century, the coif was usually tight fitting and of coloured, white, and often black cotton, sometimes tied under the chin with a small bow in front. Only in Alsace and Lindhorst in Schaumburg-Lippe was the coif of the full-crown and long-frill type. Alsace also featured a graceful coif with a broad bow at the back with long ends. Further north the coif became a curious sort of hood, high-pointed but flat at the apex and often covered with a kerchief tied under the chin. A cylindrical bonnet-shaped coif was much worn, very similar to some worn in Norway. Germany and Switzerland shared a head-dress the origin of which it is difficult to trace. A small round kind of pill-box placed flat on top of the head, it very often was red with broad black ribbon hanging from it. Sometimes it was more oblong in shape and placed at the back of the head, which makes one think it was possibly derived from early nineteenth-century small French hats. A *henin*-type coif survived in Schaumburg-Lippe[1], and a wimple topped with a high-crowned broad-brimmed hat reminiscent of the seventeenth century was worn in Kleines Walsertal. In the Black Forest in the twentieth century could be seen both a high bonnet topped by a ribbon and broad bands of ribbons which were tied under the chin and hung down at the back, and also the well known hat of straw trimmed with scarlet or black pompoms. Both these headgears were most likely of bourgeois origin, the hat being probably a copy of the ostrich-feather-covered hat much worn by fashionable women in the late nineteenth century. Special coifs for holy communion and high, round, flower-trimmed and beribboned marriage crowns were also worn in many parts of the country.

In Austria a pointed hood with a furred edge of seventeenth-century origin was worn, and in Montafon the head-dress, a round black furred ball, very much resembled one worn in the mid-seventeenth century by Hollar's Bohemian countrywoman; another from the same district has a look of the old bridal crown.

In Switzerland at the end of the eighteenth century there was a great variety of coifs, and her neighbour France had a big influence on those of French Switzerland, especially in the use of tulle and fine lace. The double mitre-like coif of Canton Schwyz was worn from the early nineteenth century until costume went out of fashion, but it is still worn for special occasions. Black tulle was also used on these wired coifs.

In German Switzerland the winged coif of Appenzell and the tight-fitting and frilled coifs of Zürich and Glarus, with their unusual ribbon fastenings, had their counterpart in the Munich district and Ulm.

Fribourg had a French and German head-dress. The French one, a very large flat hat, edged with a deep lace frill, reappeared in a slightly

1. *Deutsche Trachten*, M. Baur-Heinhold

different form in a special ladies dress in the Hoorn district of the Netherlands.

The German section of Swiss Fribourg had the cylindrical headgear so much worn in Germany and Norway. The bride's head-dress from Hallau was this shape.

Straw hats were very popular in Switzerland as in other countries, but the Swiss variety were gaily decorated with flowers and remained in fashion until regional costume disappeared.

The peasants of Italian Switzerland wore the medieval veil-like head-dress used so much in parts of Italy.

The Netherlands coifs of the early eighteenth century, small, tight fitting and framing the face, were already becoming regional, for instance the conical coif with its fitting forehead band, worn in Molkwerum, West Friesland province[1], descended to the Volendam women, and though the former costume has vanished, the inhabitants of this well-known village wear an identical black version for everyday. Formerly it was worn under a winged lace and linen coif, but this is rapidly disappearing and only the black pointed coif is generally worn.

Both the conical coif and the winged coif were worn by the Dutch-Danish Amager women, who came from this province.

The Marken head-dress of the early eighteenth century seems to have been a tight coif which was worn over the long hair peculiar to Marken; this hair was worn loose, not in ringlets as it is now. The cylinder type head-dress, with a flat top and reminiscent of the six-teenth-century *henin*-type of headgear worn by Breton countrywomen[2], appears in prints of the mid-nineteenth century, but may have been worn earlier. At the end of the century and at the present time this head-dress is less stiff, but shows much of its early origin.

The Hindeloopen head-dress as worn in the eighteenth century and until it disappeared in 1870 also had this *henin* look, but with a strange forward band, which is only to be found in the early Spanish Basque and Iceland coifs. This unique and interesting coif was covered with muslin and then with patterned and coloured painted calico brought to this Zuyder Zee town from India by the Dutch East Indies Company. In the eighteenth and nineteenth centuries the Dutch coifs in general were tight-fitting with curved wings framing the face. In the more northern provinces there was a net and lace or cambric and lace coif worn over a coloured cotton under-cap. The head-dress became more varied and regional in the second half of the eighteenth century and even more so in the following century until the rural costume declined during the present century.

In several villages the coif had a goffered edge, which was starched; this is particularly Dutch in style. There was a certain amount of

1. P. van der Berge. Print Room. Rijksmuseum, Amsterdam.
2. Weiditz, *Trachtenbuch*, 1527-31.

influence from fashionable coifs, especially noticeable in provinces bordering on Belgium.

In the southern part of the country, especially in Zeeland, where the regional costume is still worn in a few places, the coifs are less stiff and, together with the dress, give the impression of having come under the softer French influence. The coifs were of linen or cambric and lace; the crown was gathered in at the back and slightly goffered. They sometimes had a gathered flounce hanging down the back or sometimes a starched flounce framing the face.

This fashion with small variations remained more or less in vogue throughout the greater part of the nineteenth century. In North Beveland the coifs developed a long flounce of costly lace and in South Beveland, as the farmers grew more prosperous, the fine lace coifs increased to an enormous size, so much so that with modern transport they are seldom worn. The under-cap, formerly used indoors or for working in, is now in general use.

Hulst, on the border with Belgium and formerly part of that country, had in the nineteenth century a cambric and lace coif with a long lappet on either side of the face, resembling those of the country districts around Antwerp and Ostend.

The universal flat straw rural hat with a flowered chintz and sometimes brocaded lining was worn throughout the eighteenth century. The small crown was now flatter and the pulled-down look more evident; there were also gay coloured ribbons at the back, two fastened to the bodice and two tied under the chin. With the high coifs of Marken and Hindeloopen these hats were not worn. In Zeeland they were particularly popular and were succeeded by a straw poke-bonnet, usually lined with blue, with long ribbons in Walcheren and North Beveland, and a small gathered ribbon at the back in South Beveland. These straw bonnets were also worn in West Friesland, where they had a more fashionable look, as they had also in the provinces near the Belgium frontier and in that country itself in the few places where they were worn in the nineteenth century.

The most unusual part of the Dutch headgear was the silver band with gold terminals of various designs adopted in the eighteenth century and worn in the previous century by bourgeois women under their wide, white, starched coifs. This band was pinned to the under-cap and had various regional and rural names. In the nineteenth century it became considerably wider in the northern and middle provinces of the country. In Friesland and Groningen it developed into a gold coif, entirely covering the head, but this was really a ladies', not a rural headgear. In Zeeland the band never widened, and because the coif covered the ears and the fashionable nineteenth-century ear-rings could not be worn, the narrow gold band had corkscrew ends from which ear-rings or "hangers" were suspended, of elaborate and beautiful design. They were regional in fashion.

In the nineteenth century the countrywomen of South Beveland wore two differently shaped coifs, one being for Protestants and the other for Catholics. These are still in existence.

Denmark's eighteenth-century coif is interesting as it retained the traditional line and was little influenced by the daintier bourgeois coif. Amager still had the conical coif with upturned edge, but by the end of the century a more cylindrical coif was used, with a narrow rolled edge. In the early nineteenth century there was a hint of the influence of the deep-crowned fashionable straw bonnet in the blue coif which extended backward, so that over it the winter shawl could be draped. On the whole the Amager coifs and caps continued to show their Dutch origin and, if not of conical shape, were tied under the chin with a bow or broad strap, the latter being more Danish than Dutch.

The modern Amager woman has a white scarf-like head-dress, which is lined with blue and bears no resemblance to the coifs of what was one of the most traditional costumes in western Europe.

Laxsoe and the coast of west Jutland in the first half of the nineteenth century had a tight-fitting round coif of seventeenth-century influence, with a scarf wrapped round the neck giving it a wimple-like effect. There is a variety of regional head-dresses. The unmarried girl in the early part of the century had a charming, gay coif, set well back on the head and tied with a wide ribbon bow. The west Jutland fishergirl had a round coif secured by a kerchief, also tied to form a wide bow, and in the same place church-going women wore a bulbous, crowned black top hat with curved brim. It is strange how these top hats crop up in countries as far apart as Denmark and Wales. Norway had a variety of regional coifs and caps, but the white linen and lace coifs with frill or flounce never developed there in the early nineteenth century. In Scandinavian countries traditional dress is still worn in two places: in Norway, by old people only, at Hallingdal; and in Denmark on the small island of Fanö.

The conical hood worn upright or sloping backwards over a tight-fitting white coif was much used, the hood being either tied behind or under the chin. In Trøndelag the women had a long tress of hair protruding from the back of the hood. Today the women of Ibiza have a similar tress coming through their kerchief at the back. In Valdres an old woman is pictured wearing a seventeenth-century balloon-type hood dyed dark blue and trimmed with a narrow red ribbon. In Voss two types of white linen coifs were worn in the late nineteenth and twentieth centuries, which with their stiffened angular appearance might have been seen in the fifteenth century.

In the late nineteenth century flowered scarves draped round the head, sometimes having the same embroidered design as the apron, had ends knotted at the back. A small bonnet-like coif, with long ends and showing fashionably arranged hair, was worn at Gudbrandsdal. In Hardanger the costume seems to have neither coif nor cap and the hair is short and modern.

In Sweden, Dalarne had the traditional Scandinavian conical hood, and Södermanland women wore an interesting wide linen coif of early shape over a red under-cap. Many of the coifs in Sweden were less severe in line than those in Denmark and Norway. They often had the gathered crown and floating frill or flounce and the hood-like coif with long side-ends and tied kerchief which were also worn in Germany and the Netherlands.

In the nineteenth century the province of Dalarne seems to have had a variety of coifs.

The flat straw hat and straw poke-bonnet do not seem to have been worn in the Scandinavian countries. The British Isles, in contrast to the rest of western Europe, never seems to have developed a regional coif, though there was a kind of rural head-dress – in Yorkshire, for example, where the coif had individuality and was not a simplified imitation of the bourgeois head-dress. Scotland was the one exception, and Wales, late in the eighteenth century, had a distinctive costume regional to the district and not a specific place.

In England the eighteenth-century rural coif had the usual round and gathered crown and short flounce framing the face. This type predominated throughout the country. Sometimes a ribbon was passed round the crown and tied with a bow on top. This headgear was simple, often with a straight piece framing the face, and was sometimes coloured. Filey in Yorkshire had a blue one.

Rowlandson's illustration to *Dr. Syntax* shows an old woman with a head-dress that has a coif-like look, with a long lappet either side of the face. In 1900 there was a "spinner" in Herefordshire who wore this type of coif.

The women of Yorkshire, and in Musselburgh, Newhaven and Fisherrow, fishing villages now part of Edinburgh, also wore a kerchief tied under the chin; that of Yorkshire was white, and those of Scotland were coloured and very much resembled those worn by Belgian women in the late eighteenth and early nineteenth centuries. When the coifs disappeared during the first half of the nineteenth century the sun-bonnet took their place for outdoor summer wear and these were worn in the remote counties of Herefordshire and Worcestershire until the beginning of the twentieth century, as was the white coif of Wales.

The sun-bonnet was a distinctive English head-dress. The so-called "mob cap" rarely figures in illustrations, though a print of 1789 in the Douce Collection[1] shows a girl returning from a hop-yard wearing one.

In the eighteenth century the flat straw hat worn over the coif was fairly universal, though Yorkshire does not seem to have adopted it. This hat, like its French counterpart had a big influence on fashionable headgear. The rural hat was trimmed with a narrow coloured ribbon with a bow in front. Occasionally the hat had a higher crown over which a ribbon was passed and the two ends tied at the back. This hat was also worn in Wales at the same time as the traditional felt hat, and before the high black hat.

The felt hat worn in Yorkshire and Wales with a fairly high, rounded crown and a brim turned down in front and up behind scarcely varies from those worn by rural women in Europe and in England since the sixteenth century.

A chip straw poke-bonnet trimmed with a wide blue ribbon seemed to be the main headgear for countrywomen in the nineteenth century, and was much worn by ths children with their scarlet cloaks. When this particularly rural headgear and the sun-bonnet vanished, apart from the kerchief worn by the Scottish fishwives already mentioned, the Welsh coifs and hats and the rare Irish hooded cloak, all vestige of rural head-dress disappeared from the British Isles.

Largely due to the writings of Jean-Jacques Rousseau and the romantic interest he aroused in nature and rural life at the end of the eighteenth and beginning of the nineteenth centuries, there was a spate of books, with excellent coloured illustrations, on the peasant costumes of various countries. These books are, I would say, on the whole fairly accurate. They most probably show the costumes as they were worn in the last half of the eighteenth century, and they created an interest in regional dress which probably caused it to retain its individuality far longer than it might otherwise have done.

This interest was shown first by the artist, the amateur artist and the historically minded, who then formed the majority of travellers. Later fast and easy travel brought the curious and staring tourists with their ubiquitous cameras, which in turn contributed to the gradual disappearance of something that was different from the general run of things. Other contributing factors were the increasing sale of cheap ready-to-wear clothes, above all the plentiful manufactured goods. Industrialised countries and those more open to outside influence were the first to abandon the distinctive rural dress.

Farmers, their families and their workers began to have enough money to travel a little, and when visiting a more distant town disliked

1. Bodleian Library

being different from the people around them, and this difference became more marked as the nineteenth century progressed.

Regional costumes mostly held their own until 1900, often until the First World War, (sometimes beyond) but the conscripted young peasants of all countries, when released from military service, did not wish to return to what now seemed to them out-of-date clothing.

The women, though they had ceased to weave and dye their own materials, remained conservative in their choice of manufactured materials, but they could no longer get the special type of goods they wanted for their regional dresses. This difficulty was even more marked in the Second World War, especially in the Netherlands, where regional dress had survived intact in many parts of the country. Another factor in the disappearance of the costumes made its appearance. Hitherto the dress of the rural people, particularly that of the working woman, had been far more comfortable than the boned, stiff corsets and elaborate clothes of the bourgeoisie and nobility. But with the coming of easy-to-wear, unboned, loose clothing among the fashionable, it was the peasant dress, with its tight corsage, long, heavy skirt, and the tight and often cumbersome coif which needed so much laundering, that was uncomfortable and less practical. This was probably the main cause of the final abandonment of the very individual rural dress, with all its flattering charm. In some countries the costumes survive for special and gala occasions, and in others the people of a few villages or districts, out of love for their traditional dress, do not mind being so different and individual amongst the welter of ready-made clothing.

With a very few exceptions it is only those over 30 years of age who wear the dress and it seems practically certain that before the century is out all trace of regional costume for daily use, with its long history, will have disappeared, anyhow in western Europe.

Luckily a large number of books and articles have been published on the nineteenth-century dress, of which there are many specimens surviving in museums, private collections and probably in farm-houses: therefore details of these costumes are not included here. There is still, however, a great deal of research to be done on the development and details of the earlier dresses. Early nineteenth-century books had excellent illustrations, but historical background was almost non-existent, as the dresses were not considered important as a part of cultural development until the end of the century. This makes all research in the subject extremely difficult; one can only be grateful to such groups of trained people in the Folk Museums of Scandinavia and the Netherlands and individual writers in Switzerland and Germany who have tackled and are still tackling this difficult task before all traces and memory of regional costume disappear amongst the people who wore it.

164. DENMARK, third to first century B.C., Bronze Age. The progenitor of all cloaks, made from dark sheep's wool. (Köhler)

165. SPAIN, twelfth century. A shepherd. Brick red cloak and hose. White tunic. (Mural in Collegiate Church of St. Isidore, León)

166. FRANCE, thirteenth century. (Chartres Cathedral)

167. BRITISH ISLES, thirteenth century: England. (Rutland Psalter)

2. Cloak, Mantle, Cape, Huik and Whittle

Men's mantles, cloaks or capes in general use

The mantle or cloak is of very ancient origin, whether it was the imperial cloak of emperors or kings, the ecclesiastical cloak, or the cloak worn by travellers and pilgrims as a protection against bad weather on journeys either on horseback or on foot: lastly – and most common of all – the all-enveloping mantle of rural men and women used not only for winter wear; in some places it was practically the only garment – a mantle by day and a blanket by night.

An early Bronze Age cloak which was found inside a Danish tomb was the ancestor of rural cloaks. It was a long kidney-shaped mantle with a long, narrow rolled collar, seamless, but fitting well on the shoulder and fastened with bronze links. The material was woven from dark sheep's wool. The *Book of Kells* (ninth century) shows a simple figure wearing a loose brown mantle with a long rolled collar. The material of this mantle is caught up in such a way as to form short but loose hanging sleeves.

The early Psalters give little or no indication as to how much the mantle was used, as their rural people are always at work, and the mantle was naturally not a suitable garment to work in, though a hooded cape – sometimes with dagged edges – is often depicted.

A twelfth-century Italian book on herb culture has figures in hooded capes; one man wears a fairly short cape with a deep hanging collar edged with blanket stitching.

A fourteenth-century picture by Gaddi shows a man wearing a long narrow cloak attached to his hood, but none of the Italian workers appear to wear the all-enveloping mantle or bell-shaped cloak.

In Norwegian frescoes of 1300, a shepherd has a cloak reaching well below the waist, leaving an opening between the edges of which the wearer's arm is passed.

A twelfth-century Spanish fresco shows an "Adoring Shepherd" in a terracotta-coloured cloak, hoodless, reaching to just below the knees and fastened on one shoulder with a big round clasp. The other shepherd has, folded over his arms, a black blanket-like garment with an orna-

168. NORWAY, *c*, 1300. Shepherd from Bergen. The gloves were unusual except in England. (Altar panel)

169. BRITISH ISLES, fourteenth century: England. Shepherd, showing the earliest form of rural gloves. (Holkham Bible)

170. BRITISH ISLES, fourteenth century: England. (Queen Mary's Psalter)

171. ITALY, fourteenth century. An amusing way of carrying his scarf. (*Tacuinum Sanitatis*)

mental border in red and white – a Celtic-like garment. This figure also wears the Celtic trews.

Weiditz, in his book on Spanish costume (1529), shows a farmer from Castile in a heavy, elaborate mantle, resembling the bourgeois gown, with wide open sleeves and a dagged edge to the hem, collar and sleeves; this same gown-like mantle was still worn in 1825 by Spanish countrymen and is illustrated in Palencia's costume book.

Goya shows three shepherds huddled in full cloaks drawn over their heads as a protection against the mountain wind; one man has a hood and a deep collar to his cloak, which is fastened in front with a round clasp.

The French peasant of medieval times does not seem to have worn the full cloak or mantle, but, according to miniatures in a late thirteenth-century Psalter and other manuscripts of this and later centuries, he did sometimes wear the hooded cape.

The cloak proper appears in the first half of the seventeenth century and was adapted from the fashionable cloak of the period. The probability is that the cloaks seen so frequently in the paintings of peasants by the seventeenth-century artists Georges de la Tour and the le Nains were cast-offs from the Feigneur and his family – not fashionable town wear but the type worn by country gentry. The le Nains, who painted many country scenes, show a variety of cloaks of heavy material, ample and reaching to below the knees, mostly with narrow turned-down collars, fastened in front with a button or clasp; sometimes the collars are cowl shaped.

Georges de la Tour's hurdy-gurdy player wears a long, ample cloak in grey-green colour, with a small turned-down collar which has narrow ends to fasten the cloak in front. There is no hood or arm opening. This type of cloak is still worn by elderly women in France in cold or wet weather.

German peasants in the early centuries wore a short or long hooded cape, but they do not seem to have worn the cloak proper.

The hooded cape was worn in most European countries and in England by rural people, especially by shepherds and travellers, but after medieval times, German, Scandinavian, Netherlands and English countrymen do not seem to have worn a cloak or mantle, and by the eighteenth century the short and long heavy coat was universally worn by men of all classes.

The loose Celtic Irish mantle is apparently the oldest of rural mantles and is linked with the Highland plaid. Both men and women wore this garment and it is dealt with later on page 105.

172. **FRANCE, 1416.** (Duc de Berry)

173. **GERMANY, 1497-1500.** Short hooded cloak. (Dürer)

174. **SPAIN AND PORTUGAL,** c. 1529. Castilian peasant going to market. (Weiditz)

175. **SPAIN, 1529.** Castilian water seller. (Weiditz)

176. SOUTH NETHERLANDS, sixteenth century. Flemish sailor. (Madou)

177. BRITISH ISLES, 1610: Ireland, Wild Irish-woman. (Speed's Atlas)

178. BRITISH ISLES, 1610: Ireland, Wild Irishman (Speed's Atlas)

179. BRITISH ISLES, 1641: Scotland. (German woodcut)

180. BRITISH ISLES, *c.* 1730: Scotland. The belted plaid and cloak (16′ x 5′). (McClintock)

181. SPAIN, 1808. Peasant of the environs of Toro, León. (Ackermann)

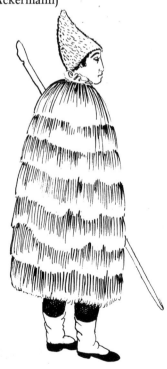

182. FRANCE, *c.* 1800: Gascony. Shepherd with white cloak and hood and red border and tassels. Brown fur long coat and trousers. Dark blue waistcoat or jacket with sleeves. Bare feet. Stilts. (Labassière)

183. PORTUGAL, 1825. Peasant in straw cloak. (Ackermann)

Women's mantles, cloaks or capes in general use

Women have always worn and still, unlike men, continue to wear this enveloping, sleeveless garment, the origin of which is very ancient. Greek and Roman peasants wore cloaks and their shape influenced the European garment, as did also the "veiled mantle" from north Africa. (The medieval funeral cloak was derived from both the African and European models. All classes of women wore the cloak. Peasant women in cold and mountainous countries wore them in winter, made of rough material. Not many manuscripts give illustrations of women in cloaks, but then the women were nearly always depicted at work. When worn this garment most likely resembled the medieval funeral cloak – long and straight, with a hood pulled over the coif as a protection against wind and rain.)

(One of the earliest illustrations is of a French bourgeoise of 1350 wearing a well-shaped cloak, fastened on one shoulder under the wimple: this particular type of cloak remained in fashion for centuries.

Hottenroth speaks of the German *Capuze,* a fourteenth-century cloak with hood.)

The early sixteenth-century Flemish *Heures de Notre Dame de Hennessey* includes a miniature of a winter scene showing a variety of cloaks – one of these, a very simple mantle-type of heavy brown material, is draped over the head and caught up under the arms without apparently any fastening. Another type, a real bell-shaped cloak with a round neck, is fastened in front and hangs to just below the hips.

The first German illustration of a sleeveless cloak I have found is in a woodcut by Beham (1520) of an old peasant couple. The woman wears a hip-length, hoodless, collarless garment fastened in front and coming to a point on each side. There are several of this type illustrated in the Flemish *Heures de Notre Dame de Hennessey.* A Hottenroth illustration. gives a sixteenth-century example which is very ample; it is caught up in front and under the arms and hangs to a deep point at the back; it has a hood – not in use as the woman is wearing a high hat. Another Hottenroth seventeenth-century illustration is of a farmer's widow whose cloak is gathered into a narrow neckband, fastened in front and without a hood.

Hollar in 1642 drew a rural woman from Bohemia in a rather elaborate example, straight, with a front edging of fur and fastened under an unusually long wimple, obviously a protection against the cold.

In Weiditz's *Spanish Voyage* of 1529, the countrywomen wear over their heads a short enveloping mantle into which they tuck their arms; there is an illustration of a similar one in a Spanish book of 1803. In a 1612 *Album Amicorum* a Spanish rural woman wears a heavy

184. SOUTH NETHERLANDS, *c.* 1520. Brown rough cloth cloak. Blue apron. Red skirt. *(Heures de Notre Dame de Hennessey)*

185. GERMANY, sixteenth century. From near Cologne (Hottenroth)

186. SPAIN, 1575: Granada. (Georgius Braun)

187. FRANCE, 1529. Woman of Roussillon. (Weiditz)

head cloak which also covers the shoulders, but this is really more of a head-dress than a mantle; a shortened version of this type can be seen in Rembrandt's etchings, and it is called in Dutch *de kappe*. In Toro, Ansolana and other parts of Spain this head-mantle was still worn in the early nineteenth century, but it was more enveloping and had something of a short *huik*.

Hollar has an illustration of a well-to-do Danish farmer's wife of 1643. She wears a bell-shaped cloak, with a narrow encircling collar, very much like the fringed collar of an Irish lady's sixteenth-century mantle. The Dutch-Danish Amager farming families who brought their costume with them from Holland to Denmark, adopted the one garment that was apparently not worn in their native province. In the eighteenth century they wore a mantle-like shawl which they wrapped tightly round their body.

In the eighteenth century Corsican women wore, draped over their heads, the long embroidered shawl much favoured by Italian women.

English rural women must have had some kind of cloak for winter, but I have found none illustrated in the early manuscript books. However, Cunnington[1] writes that "hooded cloaks with Orillettes" and small wimples were worn in the early fourteenth century for travelling.

Baldwin in his *Sumptuary Laws of Legislation of England* states that in the fourteenth century cloaks, wooden soled shoes and gloves were worn by the "lower classes", but this probably refers to countrymen. Countrywomen probably travelled very little; even today there are old peasants in Holland who have never been in or seen a train.

English prints of the sixteenth and seventeenth centuries never show a mantle or cloak, but as prints of rural costume of this time are very scarce, it does not signify that cloaks were not worn. By the middle of the eighteenth century the countrywoman's hooded cloak became her distinguishing garment and continued to be worn in England until the middle of the nineteenth century, in Wales until the end of the century, and in southern Ireland it is still in use.

In England ladies of the early eighteenth century wore long cloaks with the big calash which could cover their high head-dresses. The large calash-hood survived into the nineteenth century in the Welsh women's cloaks, the hoods being drawn up over the high hats and sometimes tied on top with narrow ribbons.

It was apparently not until the middle of the eighteenth century that the cloak with medium hood was generally adopted by countrywomen, and it was usually of red, black, blue or brown cloth or wool. It is, however, the red cloak which is indigenous to England, Wales, the Lowlands of Scotland and the Channel Islands. Rural cloaks were worn

1. *Handbook of English Medieval Costume.*

188. ITALY, 1590. The Roman-type veil. (Vecellio)

189. GERMANY, 1739. Wedding cloak from Westphalia. (Mygdal)

190. BRITISH ISLES, 1644: Ireland. Very dark cloak of a bourgeois style. (Hollar)

191. GERMANY, seventeenth to nineteenth centuries. (Helm)

generally in western Europe, but the scarlet cloak and its predecessor, the red whittle were garments peculiar to the British Isles.

Strutt[1] gives a possible origin of these cloaks. He writes: "The crocca was a large, long cloak, open before, pleated, reaching to the ground, resembling the ecclesiastical cape but without a hood. It was used by cardinals and for that reason lost its original name and was called a 'Cardinal'. It is a winter garment, worn in the country to the present day, but in my memory had a hood annexed to it and its colour was bright scarlet."

Stuart Maxwell says, in his *Scottish Costume*, that in 1780 women wore a hooded cloak of a lustrous red, a Cardinal Cloak, as their dress for special occasions.

Peter Kalm, the Swedish traveller, notes that in 1748 "the English countrywoman when she goes out visiting wears a scarlet cloak and for every day a sort of brown manteau (Mantle) made of brownish camelot."

The red cloak is also known as the Hereford Cloak and Mary Leathers, in her *Folk-Lore of Herefordshire* (1912) writes: "In 1905 a nonagenarian recounted of the selling of wives by the country people", and in one case relates how "she stood looking down, and I thought she was admiring her own scarlet cloak."

Lady Cardigan, wife of the famous nineteenth-century Lord Cardigan presented to each girl on their estate of Deene and Deenethorpe a new dress and a red cloak with hood. Both in Wales and Jersey there are legends that during Napoleonic times French invasions were halted because French soldiers mistook the scarlet-cloaked women assembled in coastal areas for English soldiers in their red coats and did not dare to land.

There are quite a few early nineteenth-century English paintings and engravings showing the scarlet cloak. William Bigg (1802) has a painting of a seated cottage woman, and her scarlet cloak, edged with white braid, hangs on a peg on the wall.

In *Picturesque Representations of the Dress and Manners of the English* (1814) the "Countrywoman" wears a scarlet cloak with a deep cape-like hood.

In Wales blue hooded cloaks were worn by Gwent girls in 1830. The Irish Anglicised cloak was often blue and hooded. A short cloak, hip length, of very heavy material and hanging straight, with a cowl-like hood, can be seen in Francis Wheatley's *Irish Fair*. A similar type in Dorset was drawn by S. Grimm in 1777. But these short cloaks were not so common as the full-length ones. The present-day cloak, worn in Kinsale, County Cork, but known as the Munster Cloak is of fine but heavy black cloth; it is very full, lined with black silk, with ruched edges, and over this is a turned down black collar, also lined with silk

1. Joseph Strutt, *A complete view of the Dress and Habits of the People of England* (1796).

192. FRANCE, eighteenth century. Peasant from near Angoulême. (St. Sauveur)

193. FRANCE, eighteenth century: Provence. The 'flounced coif' and winter jacket. (St. Sauveur)

194. DENMARK, 1807: Amager. A winter cloak. (Mygdal)

195. BELGIUM, 1830. (Madou)

196. BRITISH ISLES, 1814: England. 'Market woman' with grey cap and deep pink gown with pannier effect. Red cloak, white apron. Grey quilted petticoat. *(Picturesque Representations of the dress and manners of the English, 1814)*

and trimmed with velvet. The cloak is fastened with wide ribbon ends, and when the hood is drawn off the head the effect is of a medieval mourning cloak.

The Belgium countrywoman of the nineteenth century also adopted the hooded cloak, known as the *kapmantel*. Madou illustrates one and also shows the *Bottresse* or Portress of Liège in hers. These women used to carry heavy baskets of coal on their backs over the high Belgian hills. A Buffa print of circa 1848 shows an Ostend woman in a long cloak, with an unusually wide hood, which was still worn in 1923.

In the 1950s a stately Dutch countrywoman from Cadzand in Zeeland-Flanders (a province of the Netherlands once part of Belgium) still wore a beautiful example, full and long, in fine black cloth with a ruched silk collar and border.

The Irish mantle, blanket, rug, whittle

One kind of mantle is of great interest both because of its origin and form. This is the "ruggy mantle" or whittle. Both names are of Scandinavian origin, but the garment itself seems to have been worn mostly by the Celtic people, and it could possibly be called a Celtic Mantle. It is often described as a double blanket or rug and in its true form it is furred.

The whittle or rug has very seldom been described; therefore I propose to give all details that I have found, and I hope more will come to light.

The New English Dictionary gives the spelling as Hwitel (OE), Hvitell (ON) and defines it as a blanket, cloak or mantle, a shawl or wrap. It is first mentioned by Boeda (900 A.D.). "He wolde his reon and his hivetleis." Then in 1000 A.D., Ælfric: "Sem and Joseph dyden anne hwitel (pallium) on hirr sculdra," and there are further mentions of the whittle in 1225 and 1393.

There is no mention of the whittle again until 1697. In a Devon will there is a bequest "To my sister Rachel my largest red Whittle." The colour is interesting as the eighteenth- and nineteenth-century Welsh whittles were red.

J. Brome in his *Travels in England, Scotland and Wales* (1700)[1] writes: "The Devonshire women have a peculiar sort of garment, which they wear upon their shoulders, they are like mantles with fringes about the edge."

One of the most interesting records of the whittle comes from *Costume of Colonial Times* by Alice M. Earle. It describes it as a West

1. British Museum Library.

197. BRITISH ISLES, nineteenth century: Ireland. Blue hooded cloak of a type still worn, and made from dark blue fine cloth. (From Kinsale, West Cork) (From a photograph)

198. SPAIN, nineteenth century. The dress for Mass: a short cloak. (Palencia)

199. BRITISH ISLES, early nineteenth century: Wales. The deep hood is to cover the high hat. (Llanover: *Welsh Costume*)

200. BRITISH ISLES, twentieth century: England. This cloak is scarlet serge. (Trinity Hospital, Castle Rising, founded in the seventeenth century)

Country garment that was apparently introduced to the U.S.A. by immigrants. "A Whittle – this was a double blanket worn by West Country women over their shoulders like a cloak." The author proceeds to give these two records: Mary Harris of New London 1655 "left a red Whittle by will". Jane Humphreys of Rochester 1668 had a whittle that was fringed. The garment became obsolete in the U.S.A. in the eighteenth century, but the name was still heard in 1894.

As the whittle seems to be connected with the West Country as well as with Wales, it may have come from Celtic Cornwall – Giraldus Cambrensis in the twelfth century speaks of the Welsh people wrapping themselves night and day in a cloak, their main garment. Whether this was the "Ruggy Mantle" of the Irish of that period, or the blanket whittle it is impossible to say: most likely it was the latter, which survived as the normal outer covering of women's wear. The Welsh whittle survived into the nineteenth century and has by its name and knowledge of its shape and colour enabled us to trace it back to its origin. For this, one must thank Ken Etheridge and his book on *Welsh Costume*. Etheridge quotes a remark from the nineteenth century mentioning "the more capacious hooded cloak as being a more practical successor to the old-fashioned Whittle". But it cost more and therefore the poorer women continued to wear the whittle for some time. The Welsh whittle was always red – in Lady Llanover's drawings brick red, but in Etheridge's book scarlet. Etheridge shows the whittle worn over the shoulders, fastened at the neck, hanging to the hem of the skirt and fringed at the ends. Lady Llanover's original drawings in the National Library of Wales give two unusual ways of wearing it. A girl from Gower wears her whittle draped over one shoulder and round her hips, apparently tied in front, fringed all round, and showing a length of skirt; another girl from the same place has her whittle twisted into a very large pad on her head with the fringed edge hanging down her back and a water jug balanced on top of this useful garment. The other Celtic mantle, the ruggy mantle (hence our rug) or Irish mantle, in sixteenth-century drawings, resembles a cape more than a folded blanket.

The word "rug", like several other words dealing with early clothing, means both the garment and the material. According to the *New English Dictionary*, the origin of the word is possibly Norwegian – *ruggeveld*, a rough woollen material, a sort of coarse frieze, a material common in the sixteenth and seventeenth centuries.

The following quotations are from the *New English Dictionary*:

1557. Any of the cloths, Kerseys, Freeces, Rugges or Cottons.
1599. Hakluyt: "People of rude condition apparelled in divers coloured rugs."

1610. "But in Ireland they shear sheep twice a year, and make of their coarse wool, rugges or shaggy mantles."
"One who wears a frieze cloak."

1611. Speed, *History of Great Britain*: "A man bareheaded, bare legged, attired in a coat of grey rugge."

1622. ". . . must be clad in Irish rugge or coarse frieze. He goes generally in winter in good thick rug and in summer most parts in a Highland plaid."

1711. *A Country man's letter to a Curate*: "A kind of make of frieze, also a frieze cloak or mantle."

Rug, a dialect word in Scandinavia, Iceland, and the Faroes (*rugg*) meant to pull. It also meant to pull hard.

Frieze was a coarse strong material with a rough nap on one side; obviously the rug was a mantle worn mostly by rural or poorer people and was of strong shaggy material.

Giraldus Cambrensis in his *Topography of Ireland and Wales*[1] (1186) says of the Irish: "They wear a small close fitting hood hanging below the shoulders a cubits length and generally made of parti-coloured strips sewn together (The Cochull Brat). Under this they use *woollen rugs* instead of cloaks." The translator adds: "The hood was probably made of the same stuff as the mantle, to describe which Cambrensis has framed the Latin word *Phalengum* from the Irish *Falad* which signifies a rug or covering of any sort. This cloak had a fringed border sewn or woven down the edges. It was worn almost as low as the ankles and was usually made of frieze or some such coarse material. It was worn by the higher classes after the same fashion, but of better quality according to the rank and means. It was sometimes made of the finest cloth with a silken or woollen fringe and of scarlet (see page 216) or other colours. Many of the rows of shag or fringe were sewn on the mantle partly for ornament, partly to protect the neck from the cold. Along the edges ran a narrow fringe of the same texture as the outer garment."

This is an excellent description of the ruggy mantle and was probably taken from Lucas de Heere's drawing of 1539[2] and the engraving from Speed's Atlas of 1610. De Heere also has a figure with a cloak draped over his head which seems to be "shaggy". Another drawing by this artist shows a woman in a mantle to her feet, draped over the arms and with a deep collar of fringe which has the appearance of imitation fur.

Another engraving from Speed's Atlas of 1610, a "Civell Woman" (bourgeois) shows her wrapped in a mantle with a deep collar which comes up to and encircles the neck. The front of this mantle is somehow looped over the bottom part of the collar and forms a wide end. The collar, the end and the bottom edge of the full mantle are fringed.

1. Translated by Sir R. Colt Hoare.
2. British Museum MSS.

The cloak worn by the "Wild Irishman" in the same Atlas has a diagonal pattern between long lines, is bell-shaped and reaches to the knee, has no collar, and is fringed round the bottom edge. The companion engraving, the "Wild Irishwoman" shows a longer and more enveloping cloak, which also has one front end pulled up, a high fringed collar and a fringed edge.

Lucas de Heere, the sixteenth-century Flemish artist, made several watercolour drawings of Irish cloaks[1]. The colours he uses for them are blue and greeny-yellow, but it is not possible to say if these were the colours actually worn or a figment of the artist's imagination. Blue was always a favourite colour for the Irish mantle and the greeny-yellow might well come from local lichen or weld dyes. Saffron being a luxury, saffron yellow was the colour most mentioned in the Sumptuary Laws as being forbidden.

McClintock[2] mentions the ruggy mantle in his book as being "worn indoors and out" with ruggy fringes and mantles of five ells of frieze wrapped round the neck, body and head by women, having no petticoat underneath. He also says: "The women of the North in 1644 had a rug doubled and belted (a belted plaid), also a brown mantle with fringe of the same date. The Sumptuary Laws had had an effect on the colour." Another mention is of a "cloak-shaped mantle" with shaggy fringe of wool like a fur collar, and poor women apparently wore white sheets when they could not afford the price of fringe.

Another writer on Irish cloaks or mantles says "they are roughly of six yards long, one and half yards broad, draped in various ways round the body when in use." The descendant of this ruggy Celtic mantle is seen in van der Gucht's drawing of a Highlander in 1743 in a belted plaid of tartan drawn up and over the arms in the same way as the "Civell Woman's" ruggy mantle, but it has a belted back, no fringe, and it reaches only to the knees and is collarless. Several of these plaids are in G. Witt's picture of "A Highland Dance".[3]

The huik (Dutch), the haik, huyke (English), huca (Latin, huque (French), die hoche (German), falie (Dutch and Flemish), kappe (Dutch)

This curious and interesting garment was in its original state a long enveloping outdoor mantle. Under a variety of spellings it meant a man's garment, a kind of short coat or cassock worn over armour in

1. Lucas de Heere, MSS Department, British Museum.
2. McClintock: *Old Irish and Highland Dress.*
3. Penicuik House, Penicuik, Scotland.

201. SPAIN, 1529-32. Street dress of Morisco woman in Granada. (Weiditz)

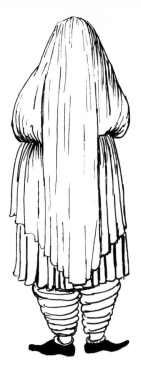

202. SPAIN, 1529-32. Morisco woman of Granada. *Huik*. (Weiditz)

203. GERMANY, 1640: Cologne. Huik. (Hollar)

204. NORTH NETHERLANDS, 1529-32. Women of Friesland. (Weiditz)

France and in place of a cloak in medieval England. It was also a woman's cloak.

To my mind the real *huik* – to use the name given to it in the Netherlands and Flanders where it was so prevalent as a winter garment – originated in north Africa. This was the *hayk* or *haik* or *hocke*. J. Taylor[1] says in 1630 of the Arab garment: "The richer sort of women wear a huiche, which is a sort of cloth or stuff plated (pleated) and the upper part is gathered or sewed together in the form of an English potlid with a tassel on." This is a fairly good description of the many varieties of the *huik*, which penetrated to certain parts of western Europe when the Moors settled in Spain.

The *New English Dictionary* gives the use of the word "haik" as early as 1350. Originally and for many centuries after, the true *huik* was not a rural garment; it needed too much stuff, and that of a supple kind to obtain the right folds and pleats. However, it ended up as the rural *falie*, an enveloping mantle worn as late as 1930 for mourning, in a village in Flanders, and still worn in its oldest form as the *stamina*, *ghonnella* or *faldetta* by Maltese women. The main characteristic of this garment is the covering of the head as well as the body, following the Moorish-Arab custom, the face being often partially hidden.

The Austrian Captain Weiditz, in the excellent woodcuts illustrating his book of Spanish costume in 1529, gives us the first clue to the origins of the *huik*. The Moorish woman wears this voluminous mantle draped high over her head-dress, leaving a band across the forehead visible, but the face in this case is not veiled. The *huik*, pulled tightly round in front, covers the arms which are wrapped in the material, so pulling it up in front, more or less like an ordinary full mantle. It is the back which is characteristic: the middle part falls in long straight folds from the crown of the head, the sides are narrowly pleated and caught up under the arms, and the whole width of the back falls in a curve to just below the knees.

Georgius Braun has, in his 1612 Atlas, a variation of the Moorish garment. The crown of the hood is flat and resembles the medieval mourning hood. The front end is thrown over one shoulder and is pleated. The Moorish women can be distinguished by their long voluminous trousers, pleated horizontally. The Spanish lady in the same Atlas wears a straight full *huik* draped over the head and topped by a round hat, with a round narrow brim, not unlike a nineteenth-century toque. A Nicholas Visser illustration has a fuller *huik* worn under a hat with a small crown and wider brim, tipped well forward. A Weiditz Catalonian woman in mourning has a *huik* gathered into a hood, and a nearly similar mantle existed in Torna, Sweden in 1827, this almost hiding the wearer's face as in the Spanish model.

1. *New English Dictionary.*

205. SWEDEN, 1827: Torna Harad. *Huik*.
(Forssell)

206. GERMANY, seventeenth to nineteenth
centuries. *Huik*. (Helm)

207. MALTA, twentieth century. Faldetta.
(People of all Nations)

208. MALTA, twentieth century. Faldetta
(People of all Nations)

The variety of *huiks* is endless. A Flemish sixteenth-century woman going to church has a voluminous black specimen mounting high over her coif. An Estremadura woman of *circa* 1640 goes to Mass in a fringed form of *huik* draped more like a shawl and almost hiding the face, but now it is developing into the mantilla (mantle), and eventually it developed into the lace mantilla. Women in the northern and southern Netherlands wore a variety of strange *huiks*. Meirvid de Kinderen-Besier[1] shows three forms in the sixteenth century, one looped up behind, under the round Spanish hat, another with a stiffened peak projecting over the forehead – this type is also found in several sixteenth-century Dutch atlases – and a strange, square, three-quarter length garment, almost hiding the face and topped by a coolie-type straw hat.

This square type of *huik* appeared in north Germany in the seventeenth century with a similar small aperture for the face. A bride from the island of Sylt in Germany has a similar one, raised high over her bridal crown. In France and Italy, though the words *huque* and *huca* were used for a kind of mantle, the true *huik* does not seem to have been worn. According to Roger-Miles in his book on French costume, a mantle with hood worn in 1350 was called a *huque*.

Mr. Duyvetter of the Open Air Museum at Arnhem has made a drawing of a lady of Waterland in a long, straight *huik* with the folds on the top of the head gathered into a frontal peak.

Today in Agueda, Portugal, a *huik*-like cloak is worn, topped by a round toque, the back of the cloak being identical with the Braun engraving of the 1612 Spanish lady. The round toque forms a soft pad on which to carry baskets, a custom which also came from the east but was used for centuries in western Europe, particularly in mountainous districts. Strutt has a note on the English *huik*. "The Huca or Hyke was originally a sort of cover which occasionally served the purpose of a veil and descended to the shoulder. In process of time it was enlarged and adopted by the men and then assumed the size and form of the mantle and covered not only the head and shoulders, but the body, a garment used to this day by the Kabihs and Arabs in Africa and the Levant."

In Malta the garment is called a *faldetta*[2], is still worn and is a true *huik*. Sir Harry Luke in his book on Malta says there is a picture of a Maltese lady in 1576 wearing one, that the name is originally Turkish and means a petticoat worn over the head. I think myself it is probably a survival of the Arab occupation or was brought to the island by Spanish ladies in the Aragonese period, because it resembles so many of the known *huik* illustrations. It is definitely an outdoor garment. If of Arabic origin it was worn to hide the wearer from male glances; if Spanish it was a garment worn for Mass or for mourning.

The *faldetta* was made in fine black cloth or silk and was worn over the

1. *Mode Metamorphosen de Kleedij ouzer voorouders in de 16ce eeuw.*
2. For further information about this garment, see *Maltese Folklore Review*, Malta, 1966.

head and arms and draped in the same way as the Moorish *huik* illustrated by Weiditz. The part covering the head had a wide-open, hoodlike appearance and was stiffened with whalebone. (Whalebone was probably also used in the sixteenth-century *huiks* to stiffen the front peaks.)

The wide curve of the head covering resembles the seventeenth-century Flemish *huik* illustrated in the *Album Amicorum* of that time, and the manner in which the top of the *faldetta* is gathered and attached to the whalebone band is identical with the *huik* worn by the early seventeenth-century Waterland lady – a long history for a curious garment. In the villages of Zabbar and Zeetien, according to Sir Harry Luke, the garment was blue and had the strange name of *xurgana*.

In the eighteenth and nineteenth centuries a variation of the *huik* was worn by countrywomen in many parts of Europe for mourning and was generally known as a *pleureuse*; in Belgium it was called a *falie* or *faaltje*. In Ryckervogel, a village in Flanders, the *falie,* a long mantle drawn over the head and almost covering the face, was worn for mourning by a woman in 1930.

According to Mynheer de Bree in his book on costume in Zeeland, the *falie* was the oldest known winter garment for countrywomen in that province and was a rectangular piece of stuff, cloth or serge, folded double with a pleat fastened on the breast by a silver or gold clasp. This garment had no head-covering.

In Denmark in the seventeenth century a cloak was worn covering the head, and fathers presented their daughters with one on their marriage.

There are a variety of expressions connected with the *huik* – for instance, "To huke" meant to cover, or, as with a *huik*, to veil or cloak. The seventeenth-century Dutch spoke of turning in the wind like a *huik*. Sir Harry Luke quotes two authors: Maurois, who describes girls wearing the faldetta like flotillas of graceful barques with black sails, and Monsieur de Lamartine in 1832 – "a half cloak of black silk, suggesting the sail of a skiff."

3. The Corset-Bodice

The corset-bodice, like the coif and the apron, was a basic garment of the rural population of many countries and long survived both the sixteenth-century fashionable stiffened *basquin* and the eighteenth-century laced and pointed bodice, worn by court ladies and bourgeoisie alike.

Before the advent of the laced corset-bodice, rural women wore a gown consisting of skirt and "body" – a bodice, but made all in one. This garment was worn up to the middle of the fourteenth century and was kept in place by a girdle or belt. By the end of the fourteenth century the bodice part of the gown, especially in Italy, had a definite fitted look, and may even have been made separately. In *Les Très Riches Heures du Duc de Berry* (1416) there was a distinct waist line. The sleeves were cut out of the body and the edges were laced or hooked close together. This remained the fashion until the body developed an entity of its own with a short or long basque: it was worn like this in many western European countries until the sixteenth century, and in Scandinavia and England until the eighteenth century.

Marie of Anjou, wife of Charles VII of France, seems to have been one of the first wearers of the tight, sleeveless, laced corset-bodice. This type of what might be called an outside corset does not seem to have become established in the taste of fashionable ladies. It rarely appears again, but the *basquin* or *vasquin*, a tight, boned and rigid bodice of Spanish origin, was very fashionable in many countries for some considerable time, developing, after 1545, a deep pointed front. This *basquin* had some influence on the shape of the rural corset-bodice, but it was far too rigidly boned and elaborate to be generally adopted by countrywomen. What they did adopt for their use was the earlier fashion of Queen Marie. As clothing was often given in lieu of wages, the peasant had a chance of sampling fashionable articles of clothing. This is very evident in a seventeenth-century picture by G. Witt *A Highland Dance*[1], in which the main dancing girl wears the fashionable low-cut, short-sleeved bodice of the period, while the rest of the dress is purely rural.

1. Penicuik House, Penicuik, Scotland.

209. FRANCE, 1416. Early lacing of gown.
(Les Très Riches Heures du Duc de Berry)

210. SOUTH NETHERLANDS, 1510. (Grimani Breviary)

211. SPAIN, mid-fifteenth century. The corset bodice is laced over an embroidered shift and *placard*. (Catalan mural)

212. ITALY, 1500. A bourgeois influence on rural Italian dress. (Lorenzo di Credi)

To return to the laced corset-bodice: the wide opening could be easily unlaced for baby feeding and was comfortable to work in, as shown by the young peasant girl going to the fields in the early sixteenth-century *Heures de Notre Dame de Hennessey*. This corset-bodice is the earliest rural example I have found. It is in scarlet cloth with a narrow white band just above the slightly dipping front edges, and is laced with cord. It is sleeveless, and held up by two straps passing over the shoulders and attached to the back. It was worn over a loose-sleeved white smock. This type of corset-bodice remained, with slight variations, practically unaltered for centuries. It is interesting to note that in this miniature the younger woman is wearing this garment while the older woman wore an old-fashioned closed and sleeved bodice.

The first illustration of the fashionable influence of the *basquin* on rural dress is a 1575-80 print in the Louvre of a French peasant. Her corset-bodice mounts high over her smock, which has a stiffened turned-over collar such as was worn by ladies in 1560. This corset also has shoulder straps, but the laced front, instead of being square as worn by Queen Marie and the Flemish girl in the *Heures de Notre Dame de Hennessey*, tapers to a deep point in front over the apron, and the edges are outlined with narrow bands, which remained in fashion. These bands were to strengthen the eyelets through which the laces passed, and to give a better pull without damaging the material.

Mila Davenport in her book[1] gives a similar mid-sixteenth-century corset-bodice from the Barcelona Catalonian Art Museum. With this corset was worn detachable sleeves fastened by ribbons to the shoulder. These sleeves were worn for gala occasions in many countries until the early nineteenth century, and in Italy until the latter end of that century.

In a Seville picture of 1500-1512 by A. de Nadales, there is a pointed front lacing, but this seems to be closing a bodice and not lacing a sleeveless corset. On the whole the Spanish women did not wear the laced corset. It was worn in Ibiza and Tenerife in the eighteenth century, but this was of rococo influence. In Italy, a warm country, the great favourite was the laced corset-bodice over a linen smock, and later, in the eighteenth century, a full-sleeved chemisette or blouse. The corset was boned. Sometimes it had a square front, though probably it often ended in a dip below the waist, but this is hidden by the apron. The arm-holes were wide and the shoulders were secured with straps or bows. With this garment were worn elaborate detachable sleeves.

The Abruzzi corset-bodice, adapted at the end of the sixteenth century, had a deep point fastened by a bow below the waist, and the elaborate shoulder straps also formed a bow.

In German Franconia in 1581 there was a low cut corset-bodice over a

1. Mila Davenport, *The Book of Costume*.

213. SOUTH NETHERLANDS, 1520. *(Heures de Notre Dame de Hennessey)*

214. NORTH NETHERLANDS, 1510. Milk maid. Hose-like long drawers and separate sleeves. (Lucas van Leyden)

215. FRANCE, 1529. Women from Limousin. (Weiditz)

216. NORTH NETHERLANDS, 1550. An influence on rural corset-corsage. (Anonymous painting)

217. SOUTH NETHERLANDS, 1559. *La Cuisinère* (Pieter Aartsen)

traditional tight chest covering, the partlet or *placard* which was also worn in the Netherlands under a variety of regional names. The Germany corset-bodice was often rigid and fitted under the breasts, without shoulder straps, and the front was edged with material. Hottenroth has an unusual illustration of a Pomeranian example of 1601, low, stiffened and worn over a *placard*-like bodice. This corset is not open all the way down, but has a small U-shaped laced opening at the top, more suited to a cold climate. The corset-bodice was worn by countrywomen in German Switzerland; Hollar has a print of one from Basle in 1643. A print of a woman in Berglen, Bavaria, shows her wearing a high corset-bodice partially covered by a falling ruff.

The laced corset-bodice was not so popular in Germany as the *Mieder*, which was also a boned sleeveless garment with wide armholes, but hooked in front. However, in the late eighteenth century, lacing again became fashionable and the corset-bodice was often worn under a jacket, as was the Austrian *Mieder*. A silver Köndler statuette of "Nancy" dated 1777 shows a deep pointed laced corset-bodice similar to the sixteenth-century *basquin*, but having a rococo look.

More rural is a Württemberg example (1790) of a corset-bodice with a very wide laced breast-high opening, with ribbon shoulder straps and fastened with a bow. This was worn over a blouse with elbow-length sleeves, a square collar and upstanding ruff.

Netherlands women wore a laced corset-bodice in the sixteenth century, very similar to the German one, over a high *placard* with sleeves. A late sixteenth-century Frisian peasant wore the *placard* with an open high collar, and this style appears in several prints and paintings. An etching by Rembrandt of a north of Holland countrywoman shows a definite regional dress with a tight, straight back to the corset-bodice, partially covered by the pointed furred edge of the kerchief. A Jan Victoors seventeenth-century painting[1] has an unusual sleeved example with wide laced opening and a top edged with fur, and showing the high *placard* suitable for a cold climate. The top sleeves reach to the elbow and there are longer undersleeves.

A Schendel seventeenth-century print[2] is of a woman from Hoorn wearing what is obviously a summer example of corset-bodice over a low cut *placard* with sleeves and undersleeves, and a deep falling ruff shaped like an open collar. Aartsen, painting in 1643, has a very low-cut example of the corset-bodice with material shoulder straps similar to those worn in Italy. Siebrechts, the Flemish painter, has a countrywoman in a square corset-bodice, low cut and over a smock-like undergarment. The corset-bodices illustrated by P. van den Berge in the early eighteenth century[3] are also low cut, laced and with shoulder straps, and are worn over tight, double-sleeved bodices, fastened down the front with

1. Wellington Museum, London. 2. Victoria and Albert Museum, Print Department. 3. Rijksmuseum Print Department.

218. SOUTH NETHERLANDS, 1565. Harvester. (Breughel)

219. SOUTH NETHERLANDS, 1565. (Breughel)

220. GERMANY, 1580: Nuremberg. (Amman)

221. FRANCE, 1575-80. Peasant girl. This style shows a strong bourgeois influence. (Bibliothèque Nationale)

bows. Under these garments the smock is visible. This costume was worn in Groningen, West Friesland and Waterland. A. Stolk's early eighteenth-century engraving shows a peasant with what was by then the regular eighteenth-century laced corset-bodice under a sleeved jacket; and a Troost print in the Douce Collection of the wedding of *Kloos en Roosje*[1] shows the girl wearing a sleeveless corset over a short-sleeved smock covered by a kerchief – an unusual style in Dutch rural costume.

In the northern Netherlands dress of the late eighteenth and the early nineteenth centuries, the hooked, basqued bodice was mostly worn but kept the low cut front of the corset. The coloured damask corset-bodice or *stiklief* worn from 1826-40 by South Bevelanders has the old traditional lines but is fastened behind, and is worn over a *placard* or *borstlap,* which has double sleeves.

Though the laced corset survived in Italy and Switzerland, it does not appear in the Dutch dress in the second half of the nineteenth century. In the twentieth century it was always the hooked, basqued bodice.

Scandinavian countrywomen apparently did not often wear the laced corset-bodice. There is, however, one illustration in Tage Hansen Nydel's book[2] which shows a Dutch-Danish Amager woman in the traditional Dutch Frisian low-cut laced corset-bodice over a high *placard* ending in a ruffed collar. Most of the Amager women wore the closed jacket of seventeenth-century Frisian origin, and sometimes a sleeveless three-quarter length coat. The Stapelholmia and Upsor women of 1612[3] also wore the short, closed bodice.

Norwegian women of the late eighteenth and nineteenth centuries wore a low-cut, sleeved bodice, fitted, and with a white front, very much like those worn in many parts of the Netherlands. A Norwegian dress of the late nineteenth century had a sleeveless corset over a white long-sleeved blouse for summer wear. The corset was not laced but fitted and had an embroidered *placard.* Hollar's (1648 print) Swedish "Girl of inferior degree" does wear the traditional laced corset, with shoulder straps, over a sleeved *placard,* and finished with a heavy falling ruff. A Dalarne dress of 1886 has a typical pointed laced corset-bodice worn over a long-sleeved blouse covered by a draped kerchief. The Swedish countrywoman also wore the *livstycke* (corset), boned and low cut like the Austrian *Mieder,* with big arm-holes and shoulder straps. It was either square or else cut high and round. It was partially hooked, but with a small opening for lacing. A Leksand woman wears a very low cut corset with shoulder straps over a long-sleeved blouse covered by a kerchief.

The laced corset-bodice was worn in nearly all parts of Switzerland, though the Johan Schemmer[4] dress of 1567 consisted of a fairly low-cut

1. Bodleian Library, Oxford.   2. Tage Hansen Nydel. *Amager, The Story of an Island.*
3. Braun and Hogenberg, *Civitates Orbis Terrarum.*   4. J. M. Vincent, in his book on the Sumptuary Laws of Switzerland.

222. ITALY, 1590. (Vecellio)

223. ITALY, 1590. The coif is based on the *bongrace*. (Vecellio)

224. GERMANY, 1660: Pomerania. (Hottenroth)

225. SPAIN, 1623-25. Typical Spanish headdress. *(Album Amicorum)*

square-necked bodice, probably all in one with the skirt and pulled over the head, having full sleeves. In the seventeenth century there are signs of a closed long-sleeved bodice. In Sennen, 1798, the corset is high, laced and pointed over a blouse with elbow-length sleeves. Josy in his book of Swiss costume (1826) says, "The German Freiburg dress was of ancient origin". Certainly it has an early sixteenth-century German look to it, with its flat *placard* trimmed with black velvet and the wide opening of the laced corset-bodice. The short jacket had also sleeves reminiscent of the sixteenth century. Women of Schaffhausen and Appenzell wore the laced corset-bodice in 1815, and the Valais women wore a laced and sleeved short jacket.

Sennen gala dress had a laced corset-bodice, wide at the top and narrow at the waist, and without shoulder straps.

French Fribourg, in contrast to the German part of the city, had a closed long-sleeved bodice covered by a wide fichu, definitely under French influence. In the early twentieth century Mittelland gala dress has a red corset of pointed *basquin* shape over a yellow *placard*, with a black velvet centre strap and black laces fastened round silver buttons. It was worn over a short-sleeved white blouse, which has at the neck the remains of the German early fifteenth-century square *placard*. This type of *placard* was also worn in the Netherlands in 1600 and in Norway in the nineteenth century.

A girl in Thurgau gala dress wears a modernised twentieth-century bodice with wide shoulder straps and laced over the traditional red placard. This is worn over a modern long-sleeved white blouse. Basel-land's Sunday dress in the early twentieth century also had a pointed black corset-bodice embroidered with red and laced in red. The back is also embroidered and high to the neck. With the bodice the girls wear a white blouse with elbow-length sleeves, and a kerchief tucked into the corset in front and pointed at the back. All of this is traditional. Basel-land working dress consisted of a brown printed cotton dirndl-type dress. The bodice was buttoned in front and had shoulder straps. With it was worn a white blouse with full elbow-length sleeves.

In France, where the corset-bodice probably originated, it was used throughout the sixteenth century. A tapestry woven in the early part of that century shows a countrywoman with a corset-bodice of a slightly earlier period, with a round and low opening, a wide laced front and the usual trimmed edges, but this corset has the long sleeves of a bodice. A French late sixteenth- or early seventeenth-century painting of peasants in the Montpellier Museum shows an unusually low cut corset-bodice with a V-shaped laced opening worn over a sleeved smock with an open collar. These corset-bodices were pointed in front and attached to the skirt at the back by a number of narrow

226. FRANCE, seventeenth century. (Louis le Nain)

227. FRANCE, 1643. A peasant woman. (Hollar)

228. SOUTH NETHERLANDS, 1664. The roll was used by rural women as a protective carrying pad. (J. Siebrechts)

229. NORTH NETHERLANDS, c. 1700: Marken. Fishwife. (P. van den Berge, Rijksmuseum)

strips of material. The very low cut, tight corset-bodice survived in various countries, even appearing in an early nineteenth-century Yorkshire dress with the same transparent and pointed kerchief partially covering the back. The 1575 Louvre peasant print has already been described in this chapter. A square type of corset-bodice was worn by a woman in the Georgius Braun Atlas (1612).

The Weiditz woodcut of 1529 of a Brittany woman shows the plain bodice of the medieval gown with short upper- and long undersleeves. The Brittany dress, though it eventually developed a variety of bodices and jackets, does not seem to have included the laced corset-bodice, except in Plougastel Daoulas. De la Tour's seventeenth-century paintings show one wide-open and laced corset-bodice, but most of his bodices have wide arm-holes and broad shoulder straps; they are very square, but not laced, and are worn over smocks with long full sleeves.

Most of le Nain's mid-seventeenth-century rural figures have long jackets over smocks, but they are closely fastened in front with a lace and are not the traditional corset-bodice.

According to Gracianne de Gardilanne and Helen Moffat in their *Les Costumes Régionaux de la France* only the Limoges and Auvergne women wore a laced corset-bodice in the late eighteenth and early nineteenth centuries.

Rural women in the British Isles did not wear the traditional low cut corset-bodice over a light smock, probably for climatic reasons; they did, however, wear a tight-fitting sleeved and laced bodice. A good example of this type was drawn by Lucas de Heere in 1574. It is tight, made of heavy material, laced over a bright red under-gown. A seventeenth-century woodcut illustrating a ballad shows a similar garment, but more pointed. Most of the bodices are square cut, sleeved and hooked in front, though several of the sleeved eighteenth-century bodices have open back lacing. The only corset-bodice somewhat resembling the European one has already been mentioned, and was worn by the Filey girls of Yorkshire in the early nineteenth century.

230. GERMANY, 1720. (Diederichs)

231. SPAIN, eighteenth century: Tenerife. (Palencia)

232. NORTH NETHERLANDS, mid-seventeenth century. This style is known as the North Netherlands dress. (Rembrandt)

233. ITALY, c. 1705-1736. Market woman of Bologna. (Todeschini)

234. FRANCE, eighteenth century. The chin clout is of a type found in various countries. (St. Sauveur)

235. ITALY, eighteenth century. (Tiepolo: fresco)

236. GERMANY, late eighteenth century: Ulm. (Hottenroth)

237. DENMARK, c. 1785. Red calico jacket showing lacing eyelets in lining. Worn by a miller's wife. (Ellen Andersen)

238. SPAIN, 1799: Ibiza. *(De mi Viná)*

239. ITALY, eighteenth century: Abruzzi. This style illustrates the elaborate embroidery. (Pinelli)

240. SWITZERLAND, 1815: Schaffhausen. (Josy) (Koenig)

241. SWITZERLAND, 1815: Kyburg. Pale blue and yellow yoke. Orange red *placard*. Pale blue bodice. White chemise. White apron with deep pink stripes. Mid blue skirt, red hem-band. Red tongue to black shoe. (Josy) (Koenig)

242. SWITZERLAND, 1815: Upper Engadine.
(Josy) (Koenig)

243. SWITZERLAND, 1815: Fribourg. Gala dress.
Marriage Crown covered in flowers. Linen
smock showing double sleeve below. Red corset-
bodice and skirt, laced over a yellow placard.
Black apron. (Josy) (Koenig)

244. AUSTRIA, early nineteenth century: Tyrol.
The *Mieder* or corset-bodice. (Lanté)

245. ITALY, 1820. Unusual side opening of corset-
bodice. (Rome)

246. ITALY, 1826. (Sezze)

247. SWEDEN, 1826. (Forssell)

248. SWEDEN, 1827: Willands Harad. An
interesting back. (Forssell)

249. SWEDEN, 1827: Willands Harad. (Forssell)

250. NORWAY, 1850. (Advertisement card)

251. NORWAY, 1850: Dordfjord. (Lexow)

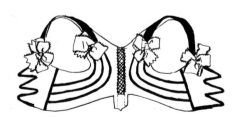

252. DENMARK, nineteenth-century corset-bodice.
   (Ellen Andersen)

253. SWITZERLAND, 1845: Corset. (Hierli)
254. SWITZERLAND, 1865: Corset. (Hierli)

255. ITALY, 1866. (Corot)

256. FRANCE, 1865: Finistère. The curious double-bodice (*Costume de Pont L'Abbé*)

257. DENMARK, *c.* 1850. Gala dress – married woman with black hairband and forehead band. Check kerchief and apron. Loose sleeves. Amber necklace. (Ellen Andersen)

258. ITALY, twentieth century: Venezia Tridentina. This dress is still worn at fêtes. (From a photograph)

4. Tunic, Frock and Smock-Frock

The continental tunic and smock-frock

What is now known, in England, as the smock-frock has as its origin a sleeved garment made of two straight pieces of material. It varied in length and was either girdled or ungirdled.

Aexel Heikel[1] traces the garment back to Egypt as a development of the apron. He says "The smock-frock was found in the Baltic provinces dating from the Iron Age."

The Greeks called this type of garment the *chiton*, the Romans the *tunica*, medieval people the *cote*, the *bliaut*, the tunic, *sloppes*, occasionally tabard, though the latter was more likely the straight-sided, sleeveless garment seen in early fifteenth-century miniatures.

The tunic was a basic garment, worn in all countries, but where the *braies* – short drawers worn under it – became breeches and the jacket and doublet made their appearance, this basic tunic became an undergarment or shirt.

Joseph Strutt says of the tunic that "it was worn by all classes of people. Put on overhead with small aperture, wearer seems to have no other garment giving such full liberty to limbs." This was probably the case with the *chiton* and *tunica*, but in medieval illustrations the *braies* are often visible. Strutt goes on to say: "Ploughmen are the only instance without a girdle, open both sides, non-free ploughman of superior rank, a free man, open on one side." I think this is very difficult to prove.

The rural tunic was worn in all western European countries both belted and unbelted, but the frock, its successor, was always unbelted, except in Italy where the *gabbanella*, the poor man's frock, was belted. When this garment, with its long history, ended up as the French and Dutch porters' blouse, it was also belted. Dutch porters were, and occasionally still are, called *wit-kiel* (white smock-frock). Hottenroth[2] says of the tunic or smock-frock of 1300 that it shows its Roman origin and that it was worn by workingmen knee-length, sleeves were long and from shoulder to wrist of "commodious width". Towards the end of the century the tunic became narrower and had a slit from the under-

1. *The Folk Costume of the Baltic Provinces* (Victoria and Albert Museum).
2. Hottenroth, *Deutsche Volkstracht*, Vol II, Chapter IV.

259. FRANCE, late eleventh century. Tunic. (Lectionary of Rheims Cathedral)

260. ITALY, 1181. Tunic. (from an early mural painting)

261. GERMANY, thirteenth century: Saxony. Early straw rural hat. (Hottenroth)

262. BRITISH ISLES, 1340: England. The rural gloves are typically English. (Luttrell Psalter)

arm and was fastened by a button.)

The *frock* was usually worn with a girdle. When the peasant wore a girdle he often pouched the tunic over the girdle, thus hiding it. Hottenroth gives illustrations of Greek, Roman, Frankish and Goth peasants in this garment.

There is also a representation of an early Christian man in the Glypthotek in Munich wearing the rural tunic. Giraldus Cambrensis has a woodcut of a country figure of the early thirteenth century in a straight tunic, the Irish *leine*. All these early tunics are depicted as knee-length or reaching to just above the knee, and all, with the exception of the *leine*, have a cord, not a belt, round the waist over which the material is looped.

The Frankish tunic has a key pattern border; otherwise it is plain.

The Greek and Roman, the Frankish and early Christian tunics have short sleeves, but the Goth tunic has long sleeves and has a V opening and small collar; the others all have round openings.

The early medieval German rural tunic is saffron coloured and is gathered into a narrow band at the neck. It is slightly longer than in earlier illustrations and has long straight sleeves.

A Spanish early thirteenth-century mural of the Adoration shows a shepherd in a very straight red tunic, with a square opening and a slit or fold starting from the belt and reaching to the knees.

A Norwegian mural from Bergen (1300) has a shepherd in a field with a knee-length tunic and rolled-up sleeves. This figure is so similar to one in the Holkham Bible both in dress and attitude (both figures wear gloves) that it seems likely that Matthew Paris painted the Norwegian murals. The Holkham Bible tunic has a V opening; the Norwegian dress is covered by a cloak. The peasant tunics of the thirteenth and early fourteenth centuries illustrated in the Luttrell and Queen Mary Psalters are also knee-length with round neck openings and long sleeves, and into the belt are stuck gloves or mittens (this glove-wearing was a typically English rural habit).

A small sickle was also placed in the belt from which hung a sheathed knife of the same type as that still carried by peasants who wear regional dress in Zeeland (Netherlands).

The Italian fourteenth-century *Tacuinum Sanitatis* has illustrations of short round-necked tunics secured with cord or belt on which the pouch was hung. Sleeves were three-quarter length, rather wide and with a split at the base.

The French peasant of the fifteenth century in the *Breviary of Philippe le Bon* was still wearing the knee-length rural tunic secured by a cord from which hung pouch and water bottle.

The French *Bedford Hours* (1423) depicts, amongst others, a blue knee-

263. BOHEMIA, *c.* 1350. Tilling. (Velislav Bible)

264. ITALY, fourteenth century. *(Tacuinum Sanitatis)*

265. ITALY, 1412. Possibly a very early smock frock. (Toesca)

266. ITALY, fourteenth century. The knee-hole stocking. *(Tacuinum Sanitatis)*

length tunic with a small revers to the front opening, long narrow sleeves, black belt and pouch. Some of the tunics illustrated are pouched over the belt, which holds the sheath-knife.

In a French late fifteenth-century tapestry the jerkin makes its appearance as a garment for rural workers, and peasants are shown working both in this garment and in the simple tunic. By the next century the latter garment has disappeared, and the tunic has been transformed into a white hempen or linen skirt worn under the jacket or jerkin. Many French and Flemish painters show peasants working in this straight-sided garment which has a side split. In the hot weather young men worked with a shirt as the sole garment, as their forefathers had in the tunic. The shirt reached to the knees and was frequently partially covered by a waist-length jerkin. When the genuine smock-frock began to appear, it was related in cut and shape both to the tunic and the shirt. Though varying in detail from country to country, it did not vary much in general outline, but was longer, fuller and with more ample sleeves than either the tunic or shirt. It was certainly from beginning to end a protective garment. It was principally worn by shepherds, and later on by waggoners and men carrying heavily laden baskets on their backs. Only in the nineteenth century was it worn more generally by rural workers, and that mostly in England. As the wearer's work had to do with care of animals, much washing was necessary. The colours were probably white, natural or blue grey.

The earliest example I can find of a garment that is definitely a smock-frock and not a tunic is that worn by an Italian shepherd boy playing a pipe in a picture from *L'Ufiziolo Visconteo* (1412). The lad is wearing a full straight frock to just below the knees, gathered into a round neck-band which is trimmed with small tabs. The sleeves are the real frock type and are gathered into cuffs.

Georgius Braun's atlases of 1582 and 1612 have two examples from the province of Limburg in Belgium. That of 1582 is a shepherd in a simple straight white garment probably made of hemp. It reaches to below the knees, has long straight narrow sleeves ending in a cuff, a tiny slit opening and turned-down collar. The second example is similar but is without collar and cuffs, and the straps of the huge basket of coal he is carrying on his back passes under each arm. This peasant porter holds by the hand his small son, who is dressed in a similar white frock, but with a narrow collar.

In a painting by van der Meulen (1689) of the siege of Luxemburg, one of the rural onlookers wears a knee-length smock-frock with a V neck and fairly wide turn-down collar and wide sleeves. The frock is the same shape as those worn in England at the end of the eighteenth century. Writing at a much later date about the Ardennes peasantry,

267. FRANCE, 1423. Sowing. Pouch and cloth for carrying seed. (Bedford Hours)

268. FRANCE, 1420-30. A shepherd. (Book of Hours, Victoria & Albert Museum)

269. ITALY, 1590. The *gabbanella*: the poor man's frock. (Vevellio)

Giovanni Hoyois in his book on the costume of this region speaks of the blouse (*trow*) of *toile bise*, "a garment pulled on over the head with two big cylinder-like sleeves. When dirty is turned back to front then inside out and then washed."

Van Bemmel, writing about Luxemburg in the nineteenth century says, "the peasant on Sundays exchanged his smock-frock for a costume with bright buttons."

J. Madou, in his Belgian book of costume (1830) shows a market with a vendor of game birds who wears a butcher-blue smock-frock (*le blouse*), very full and knee-length, low set and full-gathered sleeves, and a turn-down collar showing a red and white knotted handkerchief.

Madou also shows a carter in a similar garment and in a print called *Son of a peasant* the boy wears a blue smock-frock. Both these garments are collarless, but are gathered into a narrow band showing the traditional red handkerchief.

The only Dutch garment that I know of that resembles a smock-frock is in the Atlas of Ottens, 1680; it is worn by a man from Haamstede in Zeeland, who carries a large fish-basket on his head. He is not wearing the fisherman's short jumper (*kis-yak* in Dutch; *casaque* or *casaweke* in Flemish). It is too long and full to be a fisherman's jumper, and it has the full cuffed sleeves of the smock-frock. The colour is dark brown, and the material looks like a coarse linen or hemp.

Normally, as far as I can ascertain, the smock-frock was not worn in the Netherlands, nor in the Scandinavian countries.

Hottenroth gives a late eighteenth-century frock from the Harz district. This is the German type which is gathered into a flat band at the neck and has no collar. A Göttingen waggoner of the same century wears a similar type, but in this case the neck is fastened by two buttons. Both garments are knee-length.

Margarete Baur-Heinhold[1] has a nineteenth-century example in a shiny black linen, with a deep V opening, revers and shoulder pieces like those always worn on the English smock-frock. The sleeves are fairly wide, with cuffs, and the garment is knee-length and fairly full. This frock is worn by a Schwalmer man and is a very elaborate affair with high upstanding collar fastened by two clasps and a cord. It has wide embroidered shoulder bands and pleated revers which form a deep V. The authoress of this book writes: "The smock-frock, which has the same cut as the shirt, was made from a width of hand-woven stuff, was pulled over the head and was embroidered on the shoulder piece and on the collar. The colours were blue, red and black with coloured embroidery."

In Switzerland the smock-frock was only occasionally worn. It was a very short version more like a long blouse and was known as the Swiss

1. *Deutsche Trachten.*

270. BRITISH ISLES, c. 1679 England. A waggoner. (From a contemporary playing card)

271. BRITISH ISLES, c. 1768-94: England. The earliest honeycombed and plaited smock-frock. (S. H. Grimm)

272. BRITISH ISLES, 1816: England. (W. R. Bigg)

273. BRITISH ISLES, 1814: England. Smock. Pale grey hat. Yellow kerchief. Blue and white striped hose with red ribbon. Brownish leggings (canvas) and breeches. Dark boots or shoes. (*Picturesque Representations of the Dress and Manners of the English, 1814*)

smock-frock. The two illustrations I have found of the Swiss garment are both from Canton Uri. The 1815 example from Koenig's comprehensive book on Swiss costume, is worn by a young man with a heavily-laden basket of hay on his back and carrying an alpenstock. The frock is a simple knee-length example with a deep V opening, long revers collar, full sleeves set high and gathered into cuffs. The Uri man's from J. Hierli's *Schweizetracht* is a later example and is much shorter. It had no collar and the low set sleeves are gathered into cuffs. The wearer also has a load on his back and carries an alpenstock. Both smock-frocks are white.

The Swiss volume of *Peoples of all Nations*[1] has a photograph of an old shepherd in the Swiss smock-frock, reaching to the hips, collarless, but with two deep bags forming breast-pockets, which are also found in the Breton frock. The Breton frock illustrated in Darjou's *Costume de la Bretagne*[2] is wide and knee-length, with low set, very full sleeves, with narrow cuffs, a very wide collar and deep breast-pockets.

In Gracianne de Gardilanne's *Les Costumes Régionaux de la France* there are two nineteenth-century versions. One is of the famous Paludier de Bourg de Batz costume and is a long, full garment gathered into a squared yoke with wide flat collar, full sleeves apparently cut in one with the yoke, and narrow cuffs. The colour is white. The other nineteenth-century example in the same book is elegant and elaborate and somewhat resembles the English models. It is royal blue, knee-length with side panels embroidered in white feather stitching. The deep V opening is edged with a white embroidered band. The loose low shoulder bands are also embroidered, and the sleeves are very full and gathered into a narrow embroidered band. The wearer has a smartly tied red handkerchief with long ends.

The smock-frock is no longer worn in western Europe, the last descendant of the *tunica* being the blue-belted blouse of the French porter, the "poor man's frock".

The English frock, smock-frock and smock

The origin of the word frock, according to the New English Dictionary is uncertain. The first record is *froc* (twelfth century) Old Friesian; *rokk*, Old Holland; *Fric*, German, adopted from *hrock*, an upper garment worn chiefly by men, a long coat, tunic or mantle.

An early English reference, according to the New English Dictionary, occurs in 1527: Lane Wills – "He gruff to Richard Fini a jackett called my frocke." A later reference, of 1649 "Another girds his frocke with a

1. *Circa* 1922.
2. *Circa* 1870.

274. SWITZERLAND, 1815: Canton Uri. Short Swiss smock-frock. (Josy) (Koenig)

275. SWITZERLAND, 1815: Canton Appenzell. Goatherd. (Josy) (Koenig)

276. NORWAY, 1850. (Lexow)

277. NORWAY, 1817: Hertzberg. (Lexow)

sure thong" is more likely to be a reference to the tunic, as the English frock was never girdled.

A third definition, again according to the New English Dictionary, is a "loose outer garment worn by peasants and workmen, an overall, more fully smock frock." An instance quoted, of 1612, reads: "The rich and the poor, even from the furd to the sweating frock."

English tunics were slit at the side or in front. When they had a slit-opening (which was not always) they were occasionally fastened by a button at the top of the slit, as were those of the Italian peasant. English tunics were made of coarse woollen or coarse hempen or linen material. The colours shown in the Luttrell and Queen Mary Psalters are mostly beige, blue and often a sort of mauvy-red (probably a light madder dye). Blue was for many centuries in England a poor man's colour.

The sleeves were sometimes three-quarter length, but were often worn rolled up. The energetic worker with a front opening to his tunic would tuck one end into and over his belt to give more freedom of movement.

The earliest illustration I have found of the English "frock", wag-goner's frock or round frock are in nos. 155 and 176 in the Roxburghe *Collection of Ballads*[1] and in *Ballad, Humour, Wit and Satire 17th century* No. 84[2]. The woodcuts used to illustrate these ballads were not cut specially for the ballads but are adapted to them and are somewhat crude, but they are undoubtedly contemporary to the costumes and are most useful in a period when little interest was taken by artists in rural costume. No. 155 is earlier than the ballad, probably mid-six-teenth-century and shows a transition from tunic to smock-frock. The man sowing seed from a pouch slung over his shoulder, wears a full-length frock, which has a rolled collar encircling the neck and long narrow sleeves, and is worn over long trousers with dagged ends. No. 176 is probably early seventeenth-century, judging by the head-dress and has the features of the typical smock-frock, for example width, turned-down collar and full long sleeves. No. 84 is a little later: the frock is still short, but the arm-holes have the characteristic width and the sleeves are long and full. An illustration in Fairholt of a mid-seventeenth-century Roxburghe ballad woodcut is of a typical smock-frock, coming to below the knees, with very full sleeves with cuffs gathered into a wide arm-hole, a fairly deep turned-down collar. Over this garment is slung a big pouch. This frock is the first to show a small amount of plaiting on the front of the garment. Some of the Roxburghe ballad engravings have a small falling ruff in place of a turn-down collar. All figures have the pouch slung on a strap across the shoulders. The figures in the illustration of the Horn Fair in Samuel Butler's *Hudibras* (late seventeenth century) wear a variety of smock-frocks of

1. Harleian Coll. No. 1. B.17.
2. John Ashton, 1883. British Museum.

278. BELGIUM, 1800-1830. (Madou)

279. GERMANY, mid-nineteenth century. Shiny cotton smock-frock. (Helm)

280. FRANCE, 1865. Smock-frock with breast-pockets. (Darjou)

281. BRITISH ISLES, nineteenth century: England. Woodman in smock-frock showing the elaborated 'smocking' of the nineteenth century. (From a photograph)

a simple tunic type with small rolled collar; the sleeves are rather narrow and most garments are hip-length. An interesting feature is the knotted handkerchief showing above the frock, which became a characteristic of the rural dress: it disappeared in the nineteenth century.

The seventeenth-century fashionable low-set sleeves and long shoulder seams influenced the smock-frock, and this fashion was retained until this garment ceased to be worn.

The set of the sleeves became lower as the loose shoulder piece became more important. The probability is that the shoulder piece was added as a protection against the waggoner's whip and the shepherd's crook, which rested on the shoulders.

The best illustration of a seventeenth-century smock-frock appears on a satirical playing car, one of an anti-Cromwellian pack[1], c. 1679, and is entitled *Skippon a Waggoner* . . . The frock is straight and rather full, worn to just below the knees. The opening reaches almost to the waist and there is a small turned-down collar. The sleeves are low-set in the true seventeenth-century fashion, turned back but with no cuffs. There is no plaiting or honeycombing. The waggoner wears the traditional knotted kerchief round his neck and a fairly high-crowned brimmed hat turned up at the sides; it is rather shapeless, as is the usual run of rural hats worn for work. His shoes are ankle-high, heeled and fastened by a rosette. The hair is fairly long, but well above the shoulder. In his hand he holds a carter's whip. The drayman, the carpenter and the cobbler in this pack wear simplified bourgeois dress. A card in another pack (probably 1700) shows a shepherd surrounded by his sheep, but this is not such a clear drawing. The shepherd wears a smock-frock to just above the knees, the opening is not so deep, and there is a slightly bigger collar. The sleeves are narrow and reach to the wrist. There is the same type of felt hat, but it is turned up in front. The shepherd carried an unusually-shaped crook.

R. Y. Swete's *Views of Devon*[2] (1788) show no rural figures in smock-frocks, whereas in the Danish artist S. Grimm's great topographical surveys (1770-1790) there are quite a few drawings of countrymen in smock-frocks, but many more in jacket and breeches, especially in the north of England. Coming to more recent times, a correspondent to *Country Life* (May 23rd, 1957) says that none is mentioned in Northumberland and Cumberland; one was worn in Warwickshire. Another correspondent to the same paper, aged 87 years, says that her husband wore his smock-frock when out beating to protect his clothes.

The most important illustration of the smock-frock is by S. Grimm, in the last quarter of the eighteenth century[3]. This one is from Dorset and unfortunately only the back is drawn. It is full, knee-length, and the

1. *The Knavery of the Rump.*   2. Exeter Museum.
3. S. Grimm 1777. (No. 15548-50 British Museum MSS.)

collar is deep, wide and pointed. This shape remained in fashion. Sleeves are full, low-set and cuffed. But the most interesting point is the first appearance of elaborate plaiting and honeycombing on the middle of the back and on the upper half of the sleeves.

From the middle of the eighteenth century many more smock-frocks were worn, and artists of this period found them rewarding garments to paint and draw. They are found in the pictures of Morland, Constable, Rowlandson and many others.

Though the majority of farm labourers shown wearing the smock-frock are either waggoners or shepherds, there are some depicted with hayfork or hoe. At the same time there are an equal number in short jackets and breeches. For a considerable period there seem to have been two types of frock, one well above the knee showing the breeches, the other knee-length or just above. Even when trousers began to be worn in the first quarter of the nineteenth century, the latter length seems to have been the favourite one – also when leggings were worn. Rowlandson paints an old man in a very long frock, a simple affair, and Constable, in a picture of *Old Sarum* has a shepherd in a knee-length frock with a plaid over his shoulder. J. T. Smith in *Cries of London* (1810) shows a carter in a long garment with deep V-shaped opening and narrow collar. In the eighteenth and early nineteenth centuries the smock-frocks seem to have no side slit or pockets. Some of Rowlandson's figures and the shepherd boy in Old Crome's *Mousehold Heath* are shown with the smock-frocks pulled up and their hands are thrust into their breeches pockets. Collars vary in size in front, but nearly all go into a deep point at the back.

After 1800 the word smock was added to frock, but the term waggonner's smock or round frock was more often used. Here a relevant reference (1841) cited by the New English Dictionary reads: "He was dressed in a coarse waggoner's frock or slop".

The colours in early and mid-nineteenth-century paintings are mostly lime-green, beige, blue or white. The earliest mention of colour is in Thomas Lodge's *Wit Miserie* (1596): "Farmer that was content in his russet frock." In 1830, according to Sally Ashten, Lobster Pot, Mousehole, Cornwall[1]: "Smock-frocks were of course off-white material. Simple honeycomb smocking at either side of yoke, in front embroidered in green thread. Large collars, one laced with green cord. Labourers and cowmen long smock frocks. Carters short to knee."

The colours mentioned in connection with smock-frocks are: (1882) Cawfield and Sawold, *Dictionary of Needlework*: "The linen from which our peasant smock-frocks are made, which is a strong green lime." (1883) Thomas Hardy: "The whitey brown ones are rarely seen afield." Mrs. Powell, Coolham: "Eighty years ago in

1. Georgina Hill, *History of English Dress*.

Ashington the farm labourer wore unbleached linen every day; dark linen on Sundays, and the name is round frock."

The older name for this type of decoration was "plaiting" and the elaborate pattern over the honeycombing was not in vogue until the mid-nineteenth century.

Though the well-known painters never bothered to show the plaiting or honeycombing, it did exist, and Pyne in an illustration to his book of costume (1808) shows a carter in a smock-frock with a back opening with a little plaiting on either side and a very deep shoulder piece with some stitching. Later in the century these shoulder pieces had elaborate patterning. *The Farmer's Boy* in *Picturesque Representations of the Dress and Manners of the English* (1814)[1] has a deep collar on his white smock-frock and also plaiting and honeycombing in front. An example painted by John Callcott Horsely, R.A., is stiff, bottle-green, heavy crash with a big collar, shoulder piece, buttoned and turned-back cuffs but no patterning. There is a very elaborate front piece of patterning to the smock-frock worn by J. T. Smith's Staffordshire man selling his wares in a London Market in 1839. And at the 1873 Michaelmas Goose Fair a country lad has an ankle-length smock-frock open to the waist in front, with a small collar and full sleeves with deep cuff. The top part of the garment is patterned to the waist. The smock-frock became far more general after the middle of the nineteenth century, though in an 1847 painting of a village choir[2] of 13 men only one wears the smock-frock. From about 1860 the plaited, honeycombed and embroidered patterns became more elaborate. A Hereford example of this period[3] is the long-waisted type and has what is now called smocking back and front and heavily patterned shoulder pieces and side flaps to the pockets.

There seems to have been no particular type, material or colour for any particular district. The same applies to the patterns of squares, whorls, and stylized flowers and leaves, nor do they have any particular meaning.

For absolute proof of a county or district pattern being regional, photographs of numerous known regional examples in museums and private hands (and there are many of them) would have to be compared to see if any particular pattern was peculiar to one district, but personally I think it was a question of fashion and individual taste and the type of pattern book used.

Hereford and Worcestershire were probably the counties that retained their rural customs the longest, and the last recorded date I can find for the wearing of a smock-frock was 1911 in the county of Herefordshire.

1. 25.7C Victoria and Albert Museum.   2. Victoria and Albert Museum.
3. Hereford Museum.

5. Footwear

Shoes made from cloth or skin

The footwear of the rural worker is by the very nature of his work simple and strong and not well cut. Until the seventeenth century it was without elaboration and very uninteresting compared to the elegant boots and shoes of the nobles and bourgeois. The result is that very little has been written about rural footwear and the names themselves are often conflicting, particularly where the wooden shoe is concerned.

Men's shoes

The twelfth-century shoe, as worn by shepherds in Spanish mural paintings of that period gives one a good idea of the origin of the early rural shoe. This Spanish shoe is a descendant of the Greek *soccus*, a shoe or sock. It looks like a thick sock, ankle high, with a rolled-over top probably of fairly flexible leather or heavy woven material. In all the Psalters and other illuminated manuscripts they are black.

In many parts of Spain the people wore the Roman *crepida,* a laced sandal; this eventually developed into the *espadrille* or *spardille* of south-west France. It seems to have been a single-soled shoe, probably oversewn like a moccasin and laced round the leg with leather thongs.

Freya Stark in her book *Alexander's Path* describes a Turkish goatherd as being "in moccasin cross-gartered like Malvolio", and this type of footwear was probably worn by early rural people. Goatskin, cowhide or roughly woven cloth were used. Amman's sixteenth-century fisherman wears a good example of this type. Material covers foot and leg up to the knee and the foot is cross-gartered, while thongs keep the leg part in place, and the top of the material forms a sort of frill. There are low wooden soles to this primitive sort of legging which was worn in several countries.

Strutt shows a twelfth-century shepherd with his feet covered in material and the ends bound round the legs like puttees reaching as high as the knee. Hottenroth's fourteenth-century north German peasant has a high shoe with the ends forming straps round the ankle and passing through a knot.

Geraldus Cambrensis' twelfth-century Irish peasant wears a *soccus*, but with a curious pointed wooden spike attached to the sole.

In many of the English Psalters and French *Livres d'heures*, the *soccus* is often pointed and reaches to the ankle and sometimes above. A medieval wall painting in Headington church shows a *soccus* rising at the back and front, dipping at the sides and fastened with an ankle-strap. This type of shoe, usually without the strap, persisted for some time in many western European countries. A Norwegian mural of 1300 has an interesting type of high shoe with a V-shaped opening held together by lacings. It is white and was probably of some bleached animal's skin.

The peasant in the French fourteenth-century *Livre de Rohan* has also a yellow skin footwear, probably goatskin, as these animals appear in the miniature. The skin of this shoe covers the foot and is tied round the ankle by a thong and then reaches a little way up the leg. It has a wooden sole and heel; the latter is unusual at this period. The skin is the colour of chamois leather.

The fourteenth-century Italian book *Tacuinum Sanitatis*, a mine of information concerning rural matters, shows herb gatherers, some wearing low boots with wide tops, others pointed shoes with two straps, square-toed shoes with one strap, and low *soccus*-type shoes. Some figures are barefooted. Obviously all are shod according to individual taste.

In 1412 an Italian had a high shoe with a banded design like one in the twelfth-century Luttrell Psalter. According to a Baldini painting a man in 1460 wore a boot with a wide open top: a similar type was worn in most western European countries during the seventeenth century. All these shoes appear to have single soles and no heels, though in a late sixteenth-century illustration there is a strapped shoe, with a thick wooden sole forming its own heel – an early example of the clogged shoe.

All through the fifteenth and sixteenth centuries the same type of low and high shoe was worn with a thick stocking of worsted or some such material, mostly in red or black and often tied below the knee.

A pair of black leather fifteenth-century boots have been dug up in Norwich. These have side openings laced by thongs, and are probably a very early example of the rural boots which were also beginning to be worn in Europe, loose-fitting with square toes and mostly with a front lacing tied with a bow.

A French rural shoe of 1498 had a dagged front flap, a fashion which reappeared in eighteenth-century Switzerland on women's shoes.

151

149

Strapped shoes were still worn in Germany in the sixteenth century with apparently single soles.

There is a very interesting anonymous French picture, of about 1600, in Montpellier Museum, depicting a rural fête which, judging from the costume, most likely was on the Belgium border. One of the men dancers shows the back of the shoe which is heavily nailed all round the sole; this nailing became a feature of the rural shoe from the sixteenth century onwards.

According to Weiditz, sixteenth-century Spanish countrymen wore two types of footwear; one was the wooden-soled sandal, which was laced to well above the ankle and was worn over a sock ending in a roll over the ends of the lacing.

The well-dressed Castilian farmer going to market wore this type in 1529 and a Palencia Navarros farmer wore an identical sandal and sock in the nineteenth century. A variation of this sandal in the sixteenth century was the *zapota*, with a thick cork or wooden sole. This was laced over the toes and heel, leaving the ankle free, and was fastened by a wide strap.

The other type, seen both in Weiditz and G. Braun's Atlas (1575) is a leather boot ending between the knee and ankle with both a narrow and wide turn-over top.

England in the sixteenth century had a square-toed, clumsy looking ankle boot, fastened by a thong in front with a fairly thick wooden sole forming a heel.

During the seventeenth century the shoes became heavier and the cork or wooden soles thicker, and they were laced in front. By this time farmers had more land to work and a heavier shoe or boot was necessary.

The high shoe or "startup" was worn in most western European countries as well as in England. There is a sixteenth-century rhyme referring to them:

> *A pair of startupps had he on his feete*
> *That laced were up to the small of his legge*
> *Homelie they were and easier too*
> *And on their soles full many a wooden pegge.*
>
> THYNNE

These pegs were obviously forerunners of the nailed sole.

Fairholt speaks of a "startup or bagging shoe". The Irish seventeenth-century brogues, according to McClintock, were a single-soled shoe, more rudely sewn than a shoe, sharp at the toe and with a flap of leather at the heel to pull them on.

Amman's 1580 fisherman has footwear similar to the Spanish peasant, a cork- or wooden-soled sandal laced high over a high sock; this was also worn by 1520 countrymen. Sometimes trousers ended in feet with soles bound with braid and attached to the shoes.

German sixteenth-century rural workers wore a high boot of leather with a fairly big turn-over, or sometimes an ankle-high shoe over hose which reached to the knee with a very wide turn over.

The popular high leather boot was worn also in the Netherlands, Spain, Scandinavia and England, and continued to be worn in the eighteenth century. Bernades illustrates one in Italy in 1815.

The seventeenth century in France was an impoverished era for the French peasant, and le Nain, who delighted in peasant scenes, often painted his rural workers barefooted or with long baggy hose or stockings covering the feet but leaving the toes bare. This type of stocking was obviously not limited to the le Nain district and was certainly worn both in and out of doors with the sabot. Wooden shoes are notoriously hard on the toes and heels of stockings.

Two innovations appeared at the end of the seventeenth century. Hottenroth illustrates a buckled shoe dated 1685; this type was for Sunday and gala wear well into the nineteenth century in the majority of western European countries, long after they had ceased to be worn by fashionable people. These buckled shoes were made of black leather and were better cut than formerly; the buckles were of brass, steel or silver according to the wearer's means. In the Netherlands especially these buckles were of very finely-worked silver in the eighteenth and nineteenth centuries and gradually developed a regional pattern, a different type for each village or district.

152

Hoyois, a Belgium, writing on costume, says that "in the Meuse country in the early nineteenth century rural men wore heavy laced shoes and only wore boots after 1850." There is an interesting little note of 1802 in *Rifleman Harris's Recollections:* "I helped my father, a shepherd, to tend his flock and herds and occasionally in the evenings to learn the art of making shoes, as I said, he was in his farmer's dress."

Women's shoes

The women's shoes are not so easy to describe as the men's, the reason being that, though women worked outdoors feeding chickens (sometimes only one precious chicken tied to a post by a string) milking goats or guarding sheep, the dresses they wore reached to their feet, and in the early illuminated manuscripts women's shoes are rarely visible. When they can be seem they are mostly the wooden-soled sandal, the patten or *galoche*. When worn, the shoes were the same as the men's, the *soccus* type and the single-soled and apparently heel-less. The skin-shoe was also worn, this consisting of a rectangular piece of skin folded up and over the foot and fastened with a leather thong threaded through a row of holes placed along the free edges of the skin. This simple type of shoe was used in Denmark in the Bronze Age, was the footwear of the Greek and Roman peasant in ancient times, and was still worn in Dalecarlia (Sweden), Estonia, and the Faroe Islands until a short time ago.

In Roger-Miles' book a 1356 print shows a French rural woman in a high shoe, wide at the top, single-soled, heel-less, with three openings through which passes a thong.

In sixteenth-century Hainault the high shoe with a top ending in a roll was worn. In Alsace the same type of shoe had a wooden or cork sole. A Flemish sandal-shoe had a folded piece of leather tied in front, leaving the sides of the foot bare (probably for summer use). The Spanish-Moorish women from Granada wore a *soccus*-type shoe and usually the high wooden *choppino* or pattens for outdoor wear.

The Danish Amager dress, which came to Denmark from Holland in the sixteenth century had a low heel-less shoe and later a fitting boot with a curved front. Faroe prints of the late sixteenth century show a leather sandal-type shoe fastened with double or single straps and also a leather sandal with a wide strap.

Those German women of the late sixteenth or early seventeenth centuries who wore skirts above the ankle showed low boots either fastened at the side with thongs or just with a side slit. In seventeenth-century illustrations they are shown carrying heavily-laden baskets on their backs and wearing stout shoes with thick wooden soles, apparently no heels, and laced in front.

In France, le Nain paints his peasant women with bare feet or in square-toed leather shoes.

The strapped shoes remained unchanged until the eighteenth century, when in most countries women either wore the wooden sabot or Dutch *klomp* or a pattern for outdoors and working in. For Sundays and feast days a leather, fashionable shoe with a heel was worn; this was ornamented with steel, silver or brass buckles and remained a rural fashion in all western European countries well into the nineteenth century or until rural dress was discarded.

Switzerland varied this type of shoe by having in front a turned-over piece of material with a dagged edge usually in red.

The Belgian women's early nineteenth-century leather shoe was of a heavier type and was sometimes laced. Where rural costume survived into the later nineteenth or early twentieth centuries a laced leather shoe of bourgeois fashion was worn for best. There are few exceptions; the women of Staphorst in the Netherlands still wear a shoe with a silver buckle on Sundays.

In the British Isles the rural women wore single-soled heel-less shoes, and in the eighteenth century strong shoes with a single-lace tie, or for special occasions buckled shoes with a thick double sole, probably of wood. According to Stuart Maxwell, in the last quarter of the sixteenth century leather shoes were worn by all classes of Scottish women, but in the eighteenth and nineteenth centuries the rural women went barefoot except for special occasions. Irish women wore the brogue or in summer went barefoot.

Walker in 1709 tells of Mary Morgan, married before the Battle of the Boyne, who wore black leather shoes fastened with thongs or string.

Welsh rural women in the late eighteenth and early nineteenth centuries wore a low-heeled slipper type of shoe in black and for work went either barefooted or with long sole-less stockings similar to those worn by German women in the sixteenth century. A strong leather shoe with a thick wooden sole and heel and a single tie in front was also worn.

Shoes made principally from wood

Clog, patten, *galoche*, sabot, *klomp*, *Holzschoe*; all these names apply to footwear wholly or partly of wood. The first three terms denote a wooden sole or hollowed out piece of wood, with a thonged, laced or leather upper strap; this kind of shoe together with those of skin formed the earliest sort of footwear for rural people.

The *salepes*, spoken of by Romans, were a kind of wooden shoe with an affinity to the clog or *galoche*. The country people strengthened them with nails.

A Harleian pamphlet speaks of the ancient *galos* and *pantouffles* and says that the early Briton made a kind of sandal-shoe held together by thongs, and that the Moors of Africa wore wooden sandals fastened the same way. Pattens were worn by Saxon women, and the *gallica* or *galoche* were Gaulish shoes with wooden soles. Priests wore wooden sandals in sixteenth-century Spain, and women the high-platformed *zapota*.

(As far as can be traced, the farmer or farm-worker in early medieval days did not wear any form of wooden shoe, though those made of skin or leather were sometimes soled with wood.)

The hollowed-out sabot or *klomp* is not seen in any of the early English, French, Italian or Flemish miniatures. This was possibly

160

because wood was then precious, being put to every kind of conceivable use, and the serf or semi-freeman would not be in the position to acquire enough solid wood of the right kind to hollow out, nor would he have the money to buy from a craftsman making such footwear. Makers of hollowed-out shoes are mentioned, but these goods were probably destined to become part of the *galoche* or patten. The word sabot was in medieval Latin *sabaudia*, probably from the Arabic *zapoto*, and is said to have been first worn in Savoy. Sometimes the sabot was confused with the *galoche*, but the two are quite different.

One reason why the history of these hollowed-out wooden shoes is so difficult to trace is that they were worn in remote country places on muddy fields, though not in mountainous districts. It is unlikely that the early painters would penetrate such regions, especially the monastic illuminators who would use as models men working around them.

Though the wooden shoe is first heard of in France, it soon moved north to the Netherlands where it became known as the *klomp*. The woods used for making these shoes were willow or poplar or other woods that do not crack. Until the eighteenth century they were worn by men only.

Thanks are due to Heer Noorlander of the Open Air Museum at Arnhem for the earliest mention I have found of a *klomp*. He quotes Lupkes as saying, in an article on East Friesland Folklore, that a certain Eggerink Beninga in 1459 ran a race to the tower of Marienkap "wherein it is spoken about *klompen* or *holscher*"; further that the *klompen* fell in two pieces.

The most interesting example of *klompen* worn by a group of peasants is to be seen in a late fifteenth-century sculpture in the Bischoplÿk Museum in Utrecht. This is an unusual piece of work as the peasants and their costumes are obviously carved from life and are not just the conventional shepherds in a manger-group. One of the men definitely wears *klompen* which are deeply hollowed out, forming a wooden heel: another man wears a heavy high boot with a front slit and no heel.

A sixteenth-century painting, the *Eierdans* (Egg Dance) by Pieter Aartsen in the Rijksmuseum at Amsterdam shows a pair of *klompen* on the floor, discarded by the dancers; these seem to be heel-less with a low back, but they are definitely not pattens, being too high in front.

The New Oxford Dictionary has an entry which is dated 1607, from *World of Wonder*: "Wooden shoes probably called sabots." The *klompen* Makers Guild of the Netherlands in 1570 had Guild brothers and numerous rules and regulations. In 1610 they asked for certain privileges, and more rules were added in 1631. From now on *klompen* must have been regular footwear for the farmers and farm-workers in the northern and the flat part of the southern Netherlands. The same applies to the French peasants' sabots, especially away from the mountainous districts.

The gardener in the illustrated book by van der Groen, 1670, wears high-backed *klompen* with toes curved upwards, which from then on became a feature of this type of wooden shoe.

There is one illustration of a heeled and pointed sabot of 1764 in Svenson's book on Swedish costume; otherwise the Scandinavian countries do not seem to have adopted the wooden shoe.

In France, by the middle of the eighteenth century, the sabot was the usual footwear for rural women; before then, as in most countries, the women wore the wooden *galoche*, patten or wooden sandal if she needed protection against rain or mud. In the eighteenth century the peasant began to acquire more land, and his wife and daughters often worked with him, so the sabot or *klomp* came more than ever into favour.

Hoyois, in an article on Ardennes costume, says that in the early nineteenth century sabots were in general use in the country but not in the mountainous regions, probably because wood would become slippery and the sabot is not easy to secure firmly to the leg, or because leather was cheap in the Ardennes. Where sabots were worn, nails were used and the insides lined with straw.

Grasset de St. Sauveur, in the eighteenth century, shows a Corsican with a sabot, and Darjou's Breton men in the middle of the nineteenth century often wore heavy sabots.

Peasants of Toro in 1808 had curious sabots with a very turned-up toe, no heel, but two long pegs where the heel should have been.

Silesia had unusual *Holzschoen* (wooden shoes) in the nineteenth century. One pair depicted are very much like those worn in the Netherlands in the fifteenth century; they have a raised bit under the ball of the foot and a square heel. Great Britain never wore the sabot-type wooden shoe, nor apparently did the Italians or the Swiss.

In the Netherlands wooden shoes were generally worn even after regional dress had been discarded. They vary in design according to the district in which they are made, though they are practically all factory-made now. They are of plain wood or are varnished a browny yellow with painted or carved designs on the toe cap. No man, woman or child in the Netherlands will come into a house with his or her *klompen* on; they are left outside the back door under cover in a neat row.

The *galoche*, patten, clog or *choppino* are all forms of a wooden sole or wooden "slip-in shoe" with or without leather thongs, straps or toe caps. The New Oxford Dictionary has a note on the *galoche* dated 1611: "A wooden shoe or patten made all of a piece, without lachet or leather, and worn by the poor clown in winter." This was probably the early English version of the sabot.

The *galoche* was the Gaulish shoe and is probably the origin of the pattens and clogs.

The patten was mostly worn by women to protect their feet from cold, wet and mud, but fashionable ladies also wore it for indoors. Pattens appear in various Italian and Flemish pictures. The Dutch call them *muilen* and they are the origin of the "mule" slipper, being often backless. Fashionable men wore them in the seventeenth century to protect their high boots from mud. Some early references to *galoches* and pattens are as follows: Langland in 1377 speaks of *galloches*, and Chaucer in 1386 says: "He were worthy to remoke his galoche." In 1572 it is referred to as a Gallage. "Patyn makers" are mentioned in 1416 and 1466. An interesting sixteenth-century engraving shows wooden pattens hanging on the wall of a patten-makers shop. A woman – obviously a countrywoman – is coming in with a pair in her hand. These pattens are not deeply hollowed out like the wooden shoes of France and the Netherlands, and they were probably only used for farmyard work.

Weiditz's Flemish lady of 1581 wears, with her winter *huik*, heel-less wooden pattens with a round toe cap.

There in 1618 print (Netherlands, *Jansonius*) in the Douce collection of a woman dancing, barefooted except for a wooden sole fastened by a narrow thong over the instep. The Guilds of *klompen-*, patten- and skate-makers were closely related in Holland.

At Polesden Lacey there is a seventeenth-century Dutch picture of a woman in wooden pattens with very thick soles, backless, with a high raised toe-cap.

In No. 91 of the *Bagford Ballads* a man is wearing what appears to be pattens with raised wooden wedges under the toe and ball of the foot, but as a long piece of wood projects from the back they may be wooden skates.

The Wenceslaus Hollar engraving of 1640 shows what was probably the first type of patten in England. It is raised from the ground by a piece of iron, with two bent ends, and is fastened by a wide leather strap over the ankle. This type of patten is worn by a countrywoman. From this date onwards they were taken into general use. The New Oxford Dictionary has a note that pattens were irons to be tied under shoes to keep out the dirt.

T. Tusser in *Five Hundred Pointes of good Husbandrie* (1573) writes: "Womens Eiers are like a paire of pattens, fit to save shoe leather in summer and to keep away cold in winter."

Kalm, a Swedish visitor to England in 1748, finds these pattens a novelty. He speaks of "A kind of wooden shoe, which stands on a high iron ring. Into these shoes they thrust their ordinary leather or stuff shoes."

Jane Austen in *Northanger Abbey* (1779) writes: "Wherever they went some pattened girl stopped to curtsey."

According to Noel Chomes' *Household Dictionary* in 1778, "Muilken" (pattens) were soles and heels of wood with a piece of Russian or other leather nailed over the top and were used by women and girls for scrubbing and spring cleaning the house. They were made in large quantities in Gelderland, a province of the Netherlands, and Munster-land in Germany and exported everywhere. Pattens were referred to in the seventeenth and eighteenth centuries as being made of the bark of trees.

In Jerosche Brockmann's book *Volksleben* there are two nineteenth-century pattens, one with a rounded toe-cap and a heel and the other a heavy "block" patten with a wide leather strap over the instep.

A. Heikel has a curious Estonian example in his book, a wooden patten with leather thongs threaded through the wood.

In Hereford Museum there are various types of nineteenth-century pattens with a ring or squares of iron under a wooden base; they are sometimes nailed with ordinary nails and they have toe-caps and straps of leather.

Reading Rural Museum also has the flat wooden patten of the same period with an iron ring, square leather toe-caps and a tied strap.

"Clog" is a purely English term and was probably applied to the wooden sole of a leather or material shoe or boot, which was worn by country people in the sixteenth century and by ladies in the eighteenth century.

Strutt uses the word clog alternatively with *galoche*. In 1737 Bell speaks of high wooden pattens or clogs. In 1759 a patent was issued for a "galosche" or clog of entirely new make.

Another New Oxford Dictionary reference is to Robert Walpole's correspondence in 1742: "I remember at the playhouse they used to call for Mrs. Oldfield's chair, Mrs. Barry's clogs and Mrs. Bracegirdle's pattens." Jane Austen in *Northanger Abbey* speaks of a fear on Mrs. Allen's part of having left her clogs. Miss Mitford in *Our Village* (1827) refers to the shawling and the clogging.

This varied terminology becomes more complicated, but as I have already said this type of footwear was originally a boot or shoe of leather or material soled with wood or possibly cork, and later, for more fashionable people, an overshoe with a wooden sole, and then in the nineteenth and early twentieth century the wooden-soled leather shoes of the Lancashire mill girls.

There was a special trade of clogging. An account for 1640 runs: "Paid for clogging a pair of clogs." In Southey's letters: "The clogger is still sometimes a separate trade from the shoemaker. A man who made clogs was called a clogger and people took their shoes to him to be clogged". Men also wore clogs, and Southey talks about clogging himself to go out into the storm. Thackeray leaves his clogs in the passage.

A clog dance was performed in England with wooden-soled shoes, and in the Netherlands *klompen* dances are still performed.

The *Encyclopaedia Britannica* describes English clogs as pattens, made with wooden soles to which shoe- or boot-uppers are attached. "Sole and heel are of one piece of maple or ash, two inches thick and a little longer and broader than the desired size of the shoe. The outer side of the sole and heel is fashioned with a long chisel-edged implement – called clogger knife or groover: it makes a groove about one-eighth of an inch thick deep and wide round the side of the sole and by means of a hollower the contour of the inner space of the sole is adapted to the shape of the foot. The upper part of heavy leather, machine-sewed, is fitted closely to the groove round the sole, and a thin piece of leather binding is nailed on all round the edges, the nails being placed very close, so as to give a firm durable fastening."

Choppinos were high wooden pattens worn by Spanish ladies in the sixteenth century, and probably earlier; they were decorated in colour. Chinese women wore the same type of patten; so do the Himalayan Sherpas of today. Certain tribes of north Africa wear them for their dances.

Cockers, gaiters, leggings, etc.

England appears to have originated the rural cockers, gaiters or leggings which became universally worn in the nineteenth century. Langland speaks of cockers, the word coming from *coccus*, a boot. They are mentioned in the tenth and eleventh centuries.

In 1681 they were made of cordwain. The Barlow sporting pictures of 1686 show the land-workers in cockers or leggings, buttoned up the side and covering the upper part of the shoe. They are described in 1811 as a kind of strong cloth or even worsted, buttoned at the side and shaped under the shoe. The word cockers is still used in the north of England for gaiters or leggings, or a combination of boot and leggings to protect the leg.

Bigg shows them, in a picture of 1820, ending at the top of the shoe and without a strap, and Allom has a pair in 1842 meeting the smock-frock and finishing at the ankle, with a fairly wide strap passing under the sole of the shoe.

These leggings or gaiters were worn mostly in England, but a costume print from Skane in Sweden has a buttoned pair of early nineteenth-century date; they button at the back and partially cover the shoe.

Darjou's book of Breton costume has a pair buttoned in front. Eekhout in an 1830 Belgian market scene shows a man selling game. He wears high gaiters of striped material, blue and white with black buttons, and they nearly cover the shoe. These cockers were the last survivors of the typical rural footwear. A rubber gum boot has replaced most of them.

6. Some Additional Items of Apparel

Aprons and naprons

Aprons and naprons, together with the coif and the corset-bodice, were the most distinctive garments of the countrywomen. In the eighteenth century elaborate lace and silk aprons for purely decorative purposes were worn by elegant women, and bourgeois women also had aprons at various periods, both as a protective garment and for ornament.

The rural apron was worn from an early period until the costume disappeared. It survived, with the coif, in the "cap and apron" of the English maidservant, which were also worn in a few western European countries, but this custom also disappeared with the Second World War, to be replaced by the small and decorative apron used by many housewives.

The thirteenth- and early fourteenth-century aprons depicted in the English Luttrell Psalter and other English Psalters were narrow and long, but stopped several inches above the hem of the skirt. They were usually white and were probably made of coarse linen or hempen with "Seckcloth", "Dowlas" or "Lockram". The English rural apron had a peculiarity of its own; it was "honeycombed" – that is gathered at the waist and overstitched with the basic stitch of "smocking" to a depth of several inches. This apron was without bib and was fastened by strings at the back.

The long narrow apron was worn in all western European countries. In most Flemish early fifteenth-century illuminated books the apron was also white, of linen or hempen cloth, a very simple affair fastened by strings or sometimes the material was cut at the top to form two narrow bands that were tied at the back. In the winter scene of the *Heures de Hennessey* one apron is royal blue and the other yellow.

The French fifteenth- and sixteenth-century aprons were fairly short and narrow and mostly white.

Italian aprons of the sixteenth century were very distinctive, long, narrow, either elaborately embroidered or else a strip of material joined together with buttons or rosettes made of material.

The German apron: Hottenroth has a tenth-century illustration of a Gaulish rural woman in a plain apron, the length the same as worn in later centuries by western European countrywomen, about 15 inches above the skirt hem. The Danish women of 1625 also wore white aprons, but these were wider and longer than in some other countries. The Swedish apron in Hollar's etching of 1643 is much the same type.

Spanish sixteenth-century aprons were often very narrow and embroidered like those of the Italian women, and one from Evigona[1] in 1623 was bunched up into a sort of pouch: this was often done by rural women, and was probably useful to keep things in.

Red and blue, as well as white, were often used for aprons and black cloth for Sundays and fêtes.

A Welsh country serving maid of 1600 had "a lynnen cloth napron" and one of black cloth and another of Welsh flannel.

Plain material was used in early times for aprons in most western European countries, but as the centuries advanced, there was more variety, especially when calico was introduced into Europe and lighter and washable printed cottons were used.

The aprons became much wider and those worn by the Italians were really elaborate, especially in the mountainous regions of the Abruzzi and Sardinia.

The Scandinavian women's aprons in the later periods were coloured cotton, white, or of finely embroidered stuff for weddings. For winter wear they were often of black embroidered cloth.

In the eighteenth and early nineteenth centuries Danish-Amager women wore pale blue aprons for week-days and white aprons for Sundays, folded into tight pleats, similar to the Dutch Marken apron of today.

The Swiss wore a good many black and red aprons in the early eighteenth and nineteenth centuries, and for gala black silk with black skirts, especially amongst the well to do; and coloured striped aprons with coloured skirts: these variations were usually regional, but not strictly so.

The Dutch aprons of this period were regional and varied. In the seventeenth century white aprons were usually worn, except for very dirty work; then they were often of heavy brown material.

In the eighteenth and nineteenth centuries aprons became gay and were made of striped or flowered, printed cottons or plain blue cotton gathered on to a deep piece of checked or flowered material; this was a very practical device as the upper part of the apron wears out first. This type of apron is still worn. In Zeeland aprons before the last war were of blue and white checked cotton, but they are now black and white. The Sunday apron is made of fine black cashmere.

1. *Album Amicorum*, British Museum.

The French seventeenth-century apron was usually white and fairly wide. In the eighteenth century it was often made of coloured and striped material for every-day use and, with some regional dresses, of heavy black material or else coloured silk. The nineteenth-century Breton women had for the Pardons and fêtes elaborately embroidered silk aprons.

The Welsh eighteenth- and nineteenth-century aprons were either of coloured checks or striped cotton, though black and white was often used.

Black silk for aprons seems to have been the favourite wear for Sundays and fêtes in the eighteenth century in Switzerland and the nineteenth century in Germany.

Aprons were often worn rolled up when the women were not cooking, and in the late eighteenth and early nineteenth centuries there was a fashion for heavy striped cotton in two different shades, usually blue and white or red and white, and the apron was folded over and taken up and fastened in front, giving a pannier-like effect. This fashion was particularly noticeable in the dress of the women of Malines in Belgium and the fisherwomen of Newhaven near Edinburgh.

In England countrywomen wore large and heavy white cotton aprons until 1900, and as long as rural costume was worn the apron formed part of it.

Attachments to clothing: *the wallet or pouch, water-bottle, sickle, knife and gloves.*

All of these were worn hanging from a girdle or belt or tucked into it. According to Cunnington, the wallets were slung from the shoulders or girdle in England in the eleventh century. (Hottenroth says that in 1400 German peasants used a wallet.) In the early French or English illuminated books I have not often found the wallet, but in the Luttrell Psalter there are illustrations of the sickle and the gloves; the latter are, as far as my research goes, peculiar to the English rural worker. The knife in a leather shield was an all purpose tool, used for agricultural purposes or for cutting bread and other foods and was used in most countries. Similar knives in similar cases of leather or silver are still carried by men in the Dutch province of Zeeland who wear the regional dress.

A fourteenth-century English shepherd from a stained glass window has a large pouch, slightly decorated, which hangs from the belt of his tunic. The Holkham Bible shepherd of the same period wears gauntlet gloves, but as his tunic is unbelted I do not know where he put them when not in use. A shepherd in an early fourteenth-century fresco in Norway is wearing a similar pair. However, these gloves are peculiar to English peasants at this period, and I am fairly certain that the painting is by Matthew Paris, a noted English fresco painter.

Knives with decorated shields were used by the herbal-workers in the fourteenth-century Italian *Tacuinum Sanitatis*. One home-going worker has an extra large pouch slung from his waist, and another, a humorist, has stiffened the end of his *lirripipe* and departs from work with his water-bottle and headscarf slung over the end.

A French rural worker, about 1423, has a black leather pouch hanging from his tunic belt. A reaper from the same manuscript has a knife in a large leather case hanging down in front. In the fifteenth-century breviary of Philippe le Bon, the rural countryman has a type of wallet which became very popular with both men and women and which survived into the nineteenth century. It is an oval pouch gathered into a round, flat top, usually of metal and was hung from a strap or chain. In the same manuscript a man has a slung, rounded water-bottle with a narrow opening, probably of pewter. A knife usually accompanied the wallet.

A fifteenth-century German reaper (from Hottenroth) has a very long sheathed knife hanging from his belt, and so has a 1581 peasant, only his is tucked into his belt; and an unusual, armed peasant of 1526 has his personal knife hanging from his belt, from which also protrudes a long sword.

The early eighteenth-century Flemish rural workers used sheathed knives, water-bottles and wallets. The wallets of the middle sixteenth century developed a new form, a gathered bag, probably of softer leather, with a strap folded under and over the belt and buttoning on to the wallet; the Flemish peasants used this kind, so did an early seventeenth-century English water-carrier and a countryman from the Danish Island of Stapelholmia at the same period. The pedlars carried their wares far and wide.

In seventeenth-century England the rural worker used a wallet trimmed with tassels. It seems to have hung from a strap slung over the shoulder, especially when the smock-frock was worn; in fact, it is never depicted with the full slop-breeches.

The Swiss seem to be the only rural people who continued to wear a leather folded pouch as late as 1815.

The sheath knife, on the contrary, remained, and a Norwegian peasant of 1809 is seen with both a fork and knife in a twin sheathed case.

Water-bottles also continued to be carried, and an English eighteenth-century hop-yard worker has also what appears to be a metal tinder box slung from his belt. An 1809 haymaker has a water-bottle slung on his back from a strap.

Another rural custom, especially in Flanders, France, England and Germany was for the sower of seed to wear a kind of white apron, which was pulled over his head with one long end hanging down in front. The man gathered up the front end of the apron in his left hand to form a sack into which he put his seed and sowed it with his right hand. The Flemish *Heures de Hennessey* has examples of this custom. Other examples are from the French thirteenth-century *Livre des Saisons* and an English sixteenth-century engraving to a Roxburghe Ballad, and a German illustration of 1622 by Martin van Cleef, only in this case the apron is tied at the back of the neck and the sower uses both hands.

A woman in a French illuminated manuscript has her chicken seed in a piece of white material tied round her waist forming a pouch at the back, and this was probably pulled to the front when needed for feeding.

A German 1522 countrywoman has bunched up her apron in front to fill with poultry seed. The rural women of western Europe from early times wore, hanging from their waist-girdle or belt, a wallet, knife, water-bottle and keys; sometimes only one item, at other times two or three.

One of the earliest examples is from the English Luttrell Psalter: it is a pouch gathered into a flat top, with the pouch end trimmed with small knotted tassels, probably to weigh it down. This type of pouch, but without trimming, was used by countrymen only in the sixteenth century: for women, however, this shape continued in use until the early nineteenth century.

After the period of the Luttrell Psalter, English countrywomen are not found with pouches or any hanging object, probably because they did not wear a specifically rural dress and did not generally work in the fields as did their counterparts in Europe.

The elegant late sixteenth-century English farmer's wife drawn by Lucas de Heere carries a pair of brownish-yellow gloves to market.

The fourteenth-century Italian women herbal-gatherers had two kinds of pouches, one nearly identical with the one depicted in the Luttrell Psalter, the other a flat pouch type, stitched with a criss-cross pattern, which was much used on men's wallets, but this one is also trimmed with bobbles and tassels.

A fourteenth-century French countrywoman from *Roman de la Rose* has a pouch gathered into a point and tied with two ends, a simple affair; and a fifteenth-century girl with a hoe, has what appears to be a metal water-bottle hanging from her waist-girdle. The 1575 Louvre engraving of a *Rustique* wears a round tasseled pouch on one side and a bunch of keys on the other, both hanging from long strap ends. In a late sixteenth-century French painting, probably painted near the Belgian border[1] the dancing peasants have pouches or rather bags of a German mid-sixteenth-century design, which consist of six oval pouches gathered into round buttons or rosettes, and in this picture they are terminated by a slightly raised flat top and are weighed down by tassels at the base.

A seventeenth-century woman from Savoy has a small pouch and knife, and an eighteenth-century Limoges peasant, a pouch and a pair of scissors. All these appendages are worn on one side and next to the apron but not covered by it.

A 1580 Bohemian countrywife has the large pouch bag already described, but finished with a silver top and hanging from a chain, and attached to it is a long sheath containing knife and fork. She carries a market-basket in one hand and a large beer-jug in the other. A Rostock haymaker of 1600 has a small pouched bag and in her hand carries a metal carrier, a traditional shape, flat, oval and narrow. The pouch and knife were still worn in seventeenth-century Germany. A Nuremberg woman of the seventeenth century has two large keys hanging from her waist, and, on her back, an enormous basket containing market goods and a big beer-jug.

A Dutch woman from Zaandam, 1700, has a small tasselled pouch and a sheathed knife; however, the German material bag with silver top, but without the small pouches, was adopted by the Netherlands countrywoman. The bag is often of rich material or beaded. Such a bag is still used today by a few peasants; formerly worn outside the apron in Zeeland, it has been for many years worn under it.

Small leather and silver sheathed knives were worn in the eighteenth and nineteenth centuries and, where the owners were wealthy, silver chatelaines, consisting of sheathed knives, scissors, watch-case and bodkin-holder were worn.

The Danish Stapelholmia, early seventeenth-century, woman with hay-fork has a water-bottle and sheathed knife, and other women from the same island a small pouch hanging on an embroidered strap. An Upsor woman of the same period has a sheathed knife and a big key.

The Scandinavian women with their eighteenth- and early nineteenth-century regional dresses do not seem to have had pouches or knives, though one late eighteenth-century woman has a small tasselled pouch on a long, elaborately trimmed strap. It hangs in an unusual place – in front and over the apron.

After the late fourteenth century Italian and Spanish countrywomen

1. Montpellier Museum. Anonymous.

and eighteenth- and nineteenth-century Swiss women do not seem to have worn pouches, bags or sheathed knives – nor did the English rural women.

Bracci or breeches

Bracci or breeches, according to Strutt, were a vesture well known to the ancient Greeks but rarely worn by them. Roman players used species of *bracci*.

The medieval *bracci* were a sort of semi-fitting drawers reaching to just above or below the knee and secured at the waist by a running thread or strap. A Luttrell Psalter boy wears a very short tunic for threshing, and his loose *bracci* or drawers come below his knee. Several men at work have only *bracci*, and a Luttrell Psalter man has his hose attached to his tight fitting *bracci* by a button.

A boy in the Headington Church medieval wall-painting wears his shirt tucked into his *bracci*, and a *Tacuimum Sanitatis* herbal-worker has a very short tunic, giving a very good view of his *bracci*, which reach to the knees. Visible *bracci* or drawers are not shown after the end of the fourteenth century, but most likely they were worn so long as the tunic-frock remained in fashion, though in many countries the long Gaulish hose or breeches were worn from waist to toes.

The bridal crown

This head-dress seems to have been worn by rural women of northern Europe, especially in Germany, German Switzerland, Norway and the Baltic Provinces, and can be linked with the Russian bride's head-dress. According to Margarete Baur-Heinhold in her *Deutsche Trachten* these crowns originated in the Middle Ages and from the Spanish court dress. The basic square and high form certainly resembles the rural *henin* as seen in many early sixteenth-century illustrations, but the flowers, ribbons and tinsel embroidery are purely Germanic. An early eighteenth-century crown from the island of Sylt consists of a high cylinder of blue, with the top decorated with silver motifs. A bride of Altenburg has an embroidered crown, cylindrical in form, topped by flowers; a Lower Saxony example is round and covered by flowers; and a high square early nineteenth-century example from Schaffhausen in Switzerland has gold embroidery. The Baltic crowns vary more. One from

Latvia is basket-shaped with a wide band and a big bow at the back, and two of them are square with metal motifs at the top resembling the Sylt crown. One example has back ribbons.

Norwegian crowns are not based on the square *henin*, but are really crown-like in shape, of metal and with elaborate motifs.

Detachable sleeves

The detachable or extra sleeve was fairly common in Italy, the Netherlands and occasionally was adopted in France and Wales. These sleeves were attached to the shoulder seam or to the short upper-sleeve by ties, ribbons, straps, or, sometimes in the Netherlands, by a skewer-like pin. One of the earliest examples is Flemish, depicted in the *Heures de Hennessey* (early fifteenth century) where an older peasant is seen eating her lunch and has a pair of red detachable sleeves pinned to the shoulder of her bodice, showing the smock through the gap. A Limousin woman from Weiditz's book of 1529 has an upper-sleeve attached to the shoulder by ribbons. It is difficult to see from Vecellio's engraving of regional dresses if the sleeves are detachable or not, as they are often covered at the shoulder with a sort of material loop or bow also worn by the French and Italian ladies of fashion. The woman in the "fashionable" rural dress from Tuscany definitely wears extra sleeves fastened at the shoulder with big bows, and the Bressano woman from a de Bruyn's engraving (1581) has a pair of detachable sleeves fastened to the deep shoulder seam of her corset-bodice. It is most likely that sixteenth-century Abruzzi women wore them, as they certainly did in the eighteenth and nineteenth centuries and into the twentieth century – especially as the Abruzzi costume hardly changed at all through these centuries.

In a painting by Domenico Tiepolo of four peasant women near Vicenza, two of them are wearing detachable sleeves; and Cipper in the early eighteenth century shows that such sleeves were always worn with the corset-bodice. For working in, the detachable sleeves were not used, only the loose sleeves of the smock are visible.

Giuseppe Azzerboni in 1790 illustrates as many as 20 variations of the detachable sleeves. A Corot painting of an Italian girl in 1870 shows the same ribbon-tied sleeves.

There is a mid-seventeenth-century Dutch market-woman whose sleeves are attached to the shoulder seam by a large skewer-like pin, obviously of wood; and P. van den Berge, the early eighteenth-century Dutch artist, has an engraving of a figure with ribbon-tied detachable upper-sleeves and tight lower ones.

173

In the eighteenth and early nineteenth centuries in Zeeland the extra sleeves were of brocade, and checked and flowered chintz; those of the island of Walcheren being elbow-length.

The dress of an eighteenth-century woman of Ibiza in the Balearic Islands has a detachable sleeve fastened in the sixteenth century manner with a material puffed bow.

It is sometimes difficult to distinguish between double-sleeves and an upper- and lower-sleeve of different materials, and the detachable sleeves illustrated in the Amager Danish-Dutch bride's dress and the Swedish Skane dress of 1800 exemplify this.

The early nineteenth-century Yorkshire "Cranberry Girl" has a green extra-sleeve; this is the only English one I have found.

Welsh detachable sleeves of the early eighteenth century and during the nineteenth century were as varied and regional as those of the Italian women and were often attached to the upper-sleeve and over an under-sleeve. As in Europe, these sleeves were worn after work.

In Hesse-Waldeck (Germany), in the nineteenth-century costume detachable sleeves were worn, but they do not seem to be general in early German regional dress.

The Water-carrier costume

Though this is not strictly a rural costume it is an outdoor costume that has been seldom described and seems to be indigenous to England. The carrier was also known as the *Paremtitii* and is so described in Georgius Braun's Atlas. In an article from *Notes and Queries*, July 1924, entitled "The Register of Malvern Priory", the author writes: "Too much should not be made of the burial of a water-carrier." At Malvern in 1551, no doubt, he carried the local water round in a barrel or bucket; this was of course the general practice.

The earliest print I have found is in the fourteenth-century Holkham Bible. The man appears to wear a tunic-frock with long sleeves. His head-dress is interesting; it is the pointed hood of the period, but is held in place by straps presumably of leather – one runs round the base of the hood just above the forehead, a second frames the face, another runs from the forehead pieces to under the chin. The effect is rather of a dog's harness. Over his shoulder and resting on his back is his wooden bucket with iron bands.

The next print is from Georgius Braun's later sixteenth-century Atlas. The carrier wears a costume of a slightly earlier period: a jerkin open down the front, with long basques to just above the knee, belted and with long sleeves with the sixteenth-century rolled pad on the shoulder seam; with this he wears a turned-down collar, long tight hose and high shoes. He carries the long wooden tankard mentioned by Ben Johnson, with bands, probably of iron or brass, which he holds by a metal handle. This tankard rests on his shoulder, supported by a long stick passing under the tankard and held in his right hand. He is bareheaded.

The most delightful drawing is *The Waterman and his dogge* from the early seventeenth-century German nobleman's *Album Amicorum: a record of travel in England*. This water-carrier wears a black leather tabard-like garment, with a pale buff doublet, full red breeches, yellow hose and white over-stockings, and heel-less black shoes. He has a flat red cap on his short hair and carries the banded tankard by the metal handle on his shoulder, but has no supporting stick, for the simple reason that in his left hand he holds the chain of his brown and white dog, who carried his master's lantern in his mouth.

The last print is from Smith's *Cries of London* (1810). Published in the early nineteenth century, the Water Carrier print is dated early seventeenth century. This man also has a tabard-like outer garment, the back is full and hangs almost like a cloak. He wears a long jerkin and full slops or breeches to the knee and strong leather shoes tied with a thong and with wooden soles. His flat cap is gathered into a band, and his hair is long and straight. He carries his tankard on a stick passing across the back of his neck. I should think this dress is about 20 to 30 years later than the *Album Amicorum* painting.

282. BRITISH ISLES, fourteenth century: England.
(Holkham Bible)

283. BRITISH ISLES, 1340: England. Very early
plaited apron. (Luttrell Psalter)

284. BRITISH ISLES, 1340: England. (Luttrell
Psalter)

285. BRITISH ISLES, fourteenth century: England.
(Queen Mary's Psalter)

7. Rural Costume in Great Britain and Ireland

England

English countrymen's dress

On the whole there was remarkably little development in the dress of the rural Englishman through the centuries, drawing as he did his fashions from those of townsfolk. Often such fashions were a generation after their prototypes and frequently they were but pale copies.

The only specific and important item of English countrymen's costume which developed over the years was the smock-frock, which has already been dealt with at some length in chapter IV.

English countrywomen's dress

The dress of the early medieval European rural woman was extremely simple, and variations of it are not easy to find. The women did not appear in the early illustrated manuscripts so frequently as men. They did work on the land, but not to any great extent in England, and their work was confined mostly to the poultry yard, milking, shepherding, occasionally weeding, and even harvesting with the sickle, and hay-making.

More work was done by women in the days when the peasants were tied to their landlords and when their homes were mere hovels, with few belongings. The spinning and weaving of their coarse hemp and linen and heavy woollen cloths and blankets was probably done during the winter days; it was a case of rising with the first light and going to bed soon after dusk: rush lights and firelight would not supply much light to work by. But as time went on, the serfs were freed and became tenants of the land-owners. The homes improved, though many were still one-storied hovels. Women then confined themselves to poultry-keeping, milking and haymaking and had more time to elaborate and embroider their clothes. Even in the sixteenth century the farmer's wife was still expected to help on the land in an emergency.

English rural clothing remained on the whole simple. The general impression is that it was neat and well-cut, of good material. One does

286. BRITISH ILES, 1574: England. Farmer's wife. British Museum. (Lucas de Herre Ms.)

287. BRITISH ISLES, seventeenth century: England. (Roxburghe Ballads)

288. BRITISH ISLES, seventeenth century: England. (Roxburghe Ballads)

289. BRITISH ISLES, seventeenth century: Scotland. (Roxburghe Ballads)

not get a feeling of great poverty from the clothes. But neither does one get the impression that rural life was a flourishing and creative affair, as one does from the costumes of some continental peasant women in the sixteenth century and onwards.

Though men's costume predominates in the old Books of Hours and Psalters, it is possible to gather some idea of the general dress of rural women both from the Luttrell and Queen Mary's Psalter of the early fourteenth century. The dress before this date remained much the same and showed little change in the main lines until the beginning of the sixteenth century.

The earliest clothing consisted of an undergarment – the smock – a word derived from the Old English word *smug* – to creep into, to put on. This garment eventually became the shift and lastly the chemise, and must not be confused with the men's round- or smock-frock, which has quite a different derivation.

This smock worn by rural women was of varying lengths and was probably woven from hemp thread. In the Queen Mary's Psalter[1] the young girls wear smocks to just below the knee, and the "Smith's Wife" in the Holkham Bible[2] has hers shorter. Her sleeves are full, whereas those in the Luttrell and Queen Mary's Psalter are tight and to the wrist.

Over the smock were worn two types of garments, one being the kirtle or gown, which was loose, sleeveless with wide arm-holes, round or slightly square neck and was drawn over the head. This garment usually extended to the ankle or just above; the smith's wife wears it just above her smock in the Queen Mary's Psalter, and the young girls have theirs calf-length.

Another type of kirtle, sometimes called the "Cote Hardie", had great width across the breast and shoulders and unusually big arm-holes, and was occasionally pleated above the waist line. These garments were contained at the waist in various ways – by the girdle to which was attached the pouch, or by the apron strings, or by a cord over which was looped the "cote" as in some Italian dresses of the period. They were also worn hanging loose.

Towards the end of the fourteenth century and in the following centuries the kirtle became more waisted and was slit down the front and then laced. The colours in the thirteenth- and fourteenth-century Psalters are red, mauvy-pink and light brown, but they would depend on what plants could be obtained locally for dyeing, which would add variety to the basic dye.

Over the kirtle was worn the apron or napron, also called by Chaucer a "balme cloth": "A balme cloth uk as white as morning myth." Only later, when the apron developed a bib was it known as a "Pinner".

1. British Museum. MSS. Department.
2. Victoria and Albert Museum Library.

290. BRITISH ISLES, seventeenth century: England. The sleeve roll is of an earlier period. Narrow apron and typical pointed seventeenth-century collar. (Roxburghe Ballads)

291. BRITISH ISLES, seventeenth century: England. Milkmaid. Note the typical banded rural skirt. (Roxburghe Ballads)

292. BRITISH ISLES, 1640: England. The early raised pattens on irons, an English invention. (Hollar)

293. BRITISH ISLES, late seventeenth century: England. Pattens. (From a photograph)

The apron was definitely a rural woman's garment, though elaborate versions were worn by fashionable women at different periods. It was probably made of coarse material such as buckram, hempen or rough, heavy linen cloth. The late thirteenth- and fourteenth-century aprons were often honeycombed from the waist downwards, about six inches in depth; the honeycombing kept the apron pleats in place and caused it to hang straight.

The honeycombing of the early aprons was eventually applied to the men's smock-frocks of the eighteenth and nineteenth centuries, and was often elaborated and embroidered. Finally it became the craft of smocking.

The head-dress of the women of the thirteenth, fourteenth and fifteenth centuries, varied, and, of course, continued to vary during the later centuries.

The young girls were probably bare-headed, as they are shown in the Queen Mary's Psalter, and as they were in western Europe. The married women had white kerchiefs or hoods, folded over the head, enclosing the neck, often with one end hanging down the back. One of the figures in the Luttrell Psalter has a round coif over her veil, and the Smith's Wife in the Holkham Bible has a round cap, with an upturned brim more like a man's cap. The kerchief-veil often hangs loose, with deep points on either side of the face. One rabbit-snaring woman in the Queen Mary's Psalter has a definite wimple pinned up at the side over her kerchief, a fashion borrowed from the bourgeois ladies' head-dress. Some of the hoods in the late fourteenth century had a point forming a *lirripipe* (a long narrow round piece of material used by fashionable men to keep their elaborate head-dress in place, but which later became peasant fashion).

Some women worked with bare feet, but most of them wore flat low shoes and probably stockings of coarse woven material.

For the small amount of travelling rural women would undertake in the early centuries, a hooded cloak was worn of coarse frieze. These cloaks were described in Chapter II. They became a distinctive rural garment, though they were also in general use for women of all classes.

The end of the fifteenth and the beginning of the sixteenth centuries yield very few pictorial English records of rural costume, in contrast to Flanders and Italy. A Flemish Psalter in the British Museum of about 1500 shows the kirtle much the same shape as in the preceding centuries, only more waisted, still round-necked, with a laced opening and short sleeves over the long tight sleeves of the smock. This was probably also the dress of the English rural woman at this period. The hood, the kerchief and the wimple were still the usual headgear. The hood at the beginning of the fifteenth century was bigger and more shaped.

294. BRITISH ISLES, 1711: England. (Tempest,
Cryes of London)

295. BRITISH ISLES, late eighteenth century:
England. Haymaking. (Francis Wheatley)

296. BRITISH ISLES, 1792: Musselburgh, Scotland.
The Scottish fishwife's dress is the only truly
regional costume in the British Isles and is still
worn. (John Kay)

297. BRITISH ISLES, early nineteenth century:
Wales. Market Woman. This woman is walking
over the hills to market and simultaneously
knitting stockings. (National Library of Wales)

It may be interesting to give a contemporary account of what was expected of a farmer's wife (whether she fulfilled all these demands is another matter).

In the *Book of Husbandrie,* by A. Fitzherbert (1523), the author, obviously a pious man with Calvinistic ideas, writes against "Prodigality in outrageous and costly array and costly raiment, against men servants whose 'cotes' be so wide that they be fayne to breche them up when they ride, as women do to their kirtles when they go to Market and other places which is an inconvenient sight[1]." Amongst the required activities of a farmer's wife, he declares that women, when they are up and ready, must sweep the house, set all things in order within the house, take up the children, array them, provide for the husband's breakfast, dinner, "souper", take malt to the mill, bake what is needed, see that the miller has the right amount of corn, make butter and cheese, gather eggs from hens, ducks and geese. "Beginning of March, to make her garden and get as many good seeds and herbs as she needeth, sow hemp to make sheets, bed-clothes, and smocks and other such necessaries, therefore let thy be always ready for a pastime that thee be not idle."

Then there follows an account of how to grow hemp, and the author continues to say what the wife must do. "Then must thou have wool of thy sheep to make clothes, blankets and coverlets. If thee have no sheep, then thee must take wool to the cloth maker . . . In time of need to help thy husband with the plough, to load hay to go to market, to sell milk, eggs, ducks and chickens." There are not a few other items listed that she must do, and the author remarks that if they have not their own wool, the woman must find something else to do. In fact it was quite a full day!

To return to the costume itself. According to a woodcut of 1552, from the *Bagford Ballads,* a felt hat was worn over a fitting coif, very much the same as is often illustrated in the Flemish Psalters of this period and also a little earlier. The shepherdess illustrated in one of the ballads has a loose-fitting jerkin-jacket with a turn-down roll collar, a full long skirt and square-toed shoes with thick soles, definitely a working dress of the period.

A sixteenth-century plaster panel at Pixton Hall, Somerset, that came originally from Nottinghamshire, is interesting for showing a transition dress. It is still a one-piece gown, but the bodice is now cut with a deep square, fastened, but not laced, to the waist. The upper part of the bodice is filled in either by a smock or a *placard* or partlet. In the Welsh sewing maid's list of clothing partlets are mentioned, and these became an important part of rural women's costume both in the British Isles and in western Europe. Even today the peasant women of Zeeland in

1. British Museum, C. 42. C. 81.

298. BRITISH ISLES, 1808 : Skye, Scotland.
(Victoria & Albert Museum)

299. BRITISH ISLES, 1820: England. Milk Girl.
An unusual corset-corsage. (T. L. Busby)

300. BRITISH ISLES, 1830: Wales. Showing the
Welsh whittle. (Lady Llanover of Gower)

301. BRITISH ISLES, 1820: England. Fisherwoman,
The house key and bread knife are similarly
carried with western European rural dress.
(T. L. Busby)

Holland often remove their bodice and work in their *buik* or partlet, which covers their chest and back.

The bodice of the Pixton woman's dress has long tight sleeves to the wrist, with a padded roll between shoulder and arm-hole. The skirt part of the gown is very full, reaches below the ankles and is partially covered with a narrow apron. The hood or kerchief has given way to a tight-fitting coif, and the hair is only visible on either side of the face.

It is the continental travellers in England who show us the most interesting rural dresses in the sixteenth and early seventeenth centuries. Fairholt mentions a Dutch traveller of 1574 who made a drawing of a well-to-do farmer's wife. Actually the traveller is a Fleming from Antwerp called Lucas de Heere, and his drawing which is in the British Museum, shows one of the most delightful and typical of English rural fashions.

I think this is the drawing that Hofnagel used in his Atlas of 1582. In the de Heere drawing one sees how the state of the rural people was improving. Baldwin in his *Sumptuary Laws of Legislation of England* says that already women had to be forbidden to wear headgear embroidered or trimmed with gold, silver or silk embroidery and had to limit the cost of materials. By 1574 such costume laws were vanishing and soon after they were abolished in England, so that it became possible for all classes to follow the fashions, limited only by the length of their purses.

The "Farmer's Wife" in the de Heere drawing has a smart, well-cut outfit. It consists of a brown gown of heavy material with laced corset-bodice, a rarity in English costume. It is laced over a red under-gown which is made visible by the wide opening of the brown upper-gown. The white linen smock worn under the gowns reaches to the neck and ends in a narrow falling ruff, which also edges the long tight sleeves of the upper-gown. A long, narrow, white apron covers the front of the gown. A flat and deep white linen collar covers the back and shoulders and is fastened in front. This deep collar in a variety of shapes was worn during the greater part of the seventeenth century and became part of the Quakers' dress. The under-gown was probably of stammel, which was the word for both red and red cloth.

The coif is the type I have named "the English coif", of white linen, simple and rounded in front and tight-fitting. Over this is worn a very smart black felt hat, with a moderately high crown, trimmed with a black ribbon band. The lady carries a pair of browny-yellow gloves in one hand and a dead cock in the other, and on her arm a basket probably filled with butter as it is covered with a white cloth. With this costume she wears black heel-less shoes. Over her mouth and chin she wears a white cloth, known as a "chin clout". This was worn at this period a

302. BRITISH ISLES, mid-nineteenth century:
Wales. (S. Cusnow Vosper)

303. BRITISH ISLES, mid-nineteenth century:
Wales. Market woman (Llanover)

304. BRITISH ISLES, Twentieth century: Scotland.
Newhaven fishwife. (From a photograph)

great deal in England and Germany and was probably a protection against the early morning mists encountered on the way to market. The *Rustica Anglicana* (English peasant) of Hofnagel's Atlas, is dressed in much the same way, only the bodice does not seem to be laced, and the sleeves are the double sleeves, and the crown of the hat is lower and rounded. One of the two figures in this engraving is shown going to market on horseback. Both these costumes have developed two characterstics of rural dress – the double sleeves, the lower one being removable when working, and the use of a band to trim the skirt, just above the hem. These two details never disappear from rural costumes whether in the British Isles or Europe.

The fishwife of the Braun Atlas and two Roxburghe Ballad woodcuts show similar dresses with slight variations in the corsage and coif. The fishwife has points to her coif and double sleeves, and one of the Roxburghe prints shows a characteristic rural chatelaine consisting of a purse and two keys hanging from the waist.

The countrywoman's effigy of 1587 in Walton-on-Thames Church has a similar gown to de Heere's woman's, but drawn in at the waist by a wide ribbon and full sleeves, gathered partlet, a fringed scarf over her shoulders and a bowler-shaped felt hat. A delightful satirical print of 1603 *At the market* shows a very standardised dress. The women are nearly all clad in fairly low-cut bodices with long tight sleeves, full long skirts and long narrow aprons. The coifs are small and vary little in shape. The ruffs are also very small; some are upstanding and some flat. Skirts are long, straight and full and the aprons long and narrow. A few women wear felt hats with rounded crowns and dipping brims. One woman, who is cleaning hard, has her apron rolled up, no ruff and bare feet; the other woman wears shoes. The lines written at a slightly earlier period might apply here: "In petticoat of stammel red and milk whitt kerchief on their heads. Their smock sleeves like winter's snow. That on the Western Mountains flow, and each sleeve with a silken band."

With the coming of the seventeenth century the conditions of the farming classes improved still more, until the arrival of the Civil Wars, which caused much distress to the rural people whose land was fought over.

The charming farmer's wife riding to market in 1623 in the album of Tobias von Schottenbach, a German nobleman travelling in England, and the brass of the wife of G. Glandfield of Hadleigh, Suffolk (1637) both show how near the rural woman's dress had come to the fashionable lady's costume.

"The Paisant woman riding on a horse" of the German album is particularly interesting because the habit at this period of riding a

305. BRITISH ISLES, 1340: England. (Luttrell Psalter)

306. BRITISH ISLES, 1340: England. (Luttrell Psalter)

307. BRITISH ISLES, 1581: Ireland. A kerne (soldier), showing an early form of kilt. (Derricke, *Image of Ireland*)

308. BRITISH ISLES, 1521: Ireland. Irish soldier in Germany. (Dürer)

horse to market by rural women seems to be particularly English and is drawn several times by foreign artists. The "paisant woman" has a huge basket of eggs firmly strapped to her big white horse. She wears a pointed bodice like the *vasquin* or *basquin* of Franco-Spanish origin, of mauvy pink, with stripes in a deeper shade of the same colour. The skirt is the same shade, the apron is blue, the falling ruff is white and the steeple crowned hat in black felt is trimmed with a ribbon band. She is certainly the forerunner of many well attired "paisants" in many countries on their way to market, which, together with Sunday church, was an occasion for a display of finery.

The other fashionable countrywoman, Mrs. Glandfield, has the same pointed *basquin* with falling ruff, but has the wide Elizabethan padded shoulders and her sleeves have turned-back ruffs at the wrist. The brim of her felt hat is wider and the crown more domed, but it is trimmed with the same type of ruched ribbon and is also worn over a tight coif.

About 1635, and worn concurrently with the Elizabethan type of dress, is a basqued jerkin, a kind of bodice, tight-fitting and open down the front with a narrow band round the waist, and with this was worn a small falling ruff. A full skirt with the "rural band" above the hem was worn with this costume. It is often seen in the woodcuts which ornament the seventeenth-century *Roxburghe Ballads*. Though these woodcuts usually bear little relation to the verses, they give a good idea of the contemporary costumes of countrywomen at a time when artists were only interested in depicting famous or fashionable people.

Again we owe to a foreign traveller, Wenceslaus Hollar, the portrait of a market-woman in 1640. She is particularly interesting as she marks a change in fashion. Her bodice is still basqued as in the 1635 woodcuts, but the sleeves are very full and set in low in the fashionable seventeenth-century manner. The falling linen collar is very deep and pointed. Her full heavy skirt with an embroidered or braided band above the hem is hitched up to show an equally heavy petticoat reaching to the ankles. She is wearing the first illustrated example of the wooden pattens which have a broad leather strap over the instep and are placed on iron supports. Actually wooden pattens had been used by the well-to-do and countrywomen as a protection against wet and mud since the fifteenth century and earlier, but the ones shown here seem to be a new type. Her coif is fairly elaborate, with a full crown, and is turned back in front and has a narrow band framing the face. She has strands of hair hanging on each side of the face, in imitation of the fashionable ringlets.

A girl from the *John Ashton Ballads* wears the Elizabethan *basquin* with the full seventeenth-century type of sleeves, deep falling collar, banded skirt, and a winged coif. This girl probably resembles the one in the seventeenth-century *Roxburghe Ballad*, "The Country Lass".

309. BRITISH ISLES, 1623-25: England. Water-carrier with protective apron of black leather. (Album of Tobias Delhafen of Nuremberg and Album of George Holzschuher of Nuremberg, British Museum)

310. BRITISH ISLES, c. 1679: England. Drayman. (From a contemporary playing card)

311. BRITISH ISLES, seventeenth century: Scotland. (Roxburghe Ballads)

312. BRITISH ISLES, early nineteenth century: Wales. 'Son of a Welsh Market woman'. (National Library of Wales, Aberystwyth)

Another Roxburghe illustration shows a milkmaid with a square-cut bodice laced to the waist, tight sleeves, a full skirt with bands probably of braid, a white apron, but no partlet or coif. She has the two short strands of hair, and on her head is balanced her milk pail. This was most likely the normal working dress of the milkmaid.

Slightly more suspect is the shepherdess in a very elaborate Elizabethan kirtle and farthingale with a *basquin* bodice, tight long sleeves, fine lawn ruff and a feathered and flowered head-dress. This is probably a design for a shepherdess in a masque.

The following ballad is a good description of the "Roxburghe girls":

A COUNTRY LASS

I think myself as good as thou
that gay apparell weare
My coat is made of comely gray
And though I keep my father's sheep
A garland of the fairest flowers
Shall shield me from the sun.
I care not for the fan or mask
A homely hat is all I ask
Which will my face protect
When we together a milking go
With pail upon our heads.

A haymaker of a Roxburghe Ballad wears a square crowned hat for her haymaking, and the lines "Give us a lass that is country bred with a paragon gown and a hat on her head", is very descriptive.

Deloney in his *Pleasant History of Thomas of Reading* talks of a country haymaker in "A red stamell petticoat and a broad strawne hat." In 1677 a countryman's sweetheart is promised "a white fustian waistcoat and a brave stammel petticoat regarded with black velvet".

Two seventeenth-century housemaids were most likely country girls, as they often are today in the countries where there is a big rural population. One illustration to a ballad shows a girl in a bodice with knee-length basque, deep collar and double sleeves, and a hooded coif tied under the chin.

The Riley painting *The Housemaid* from the Queen's collection depicts the tight coif, deep-pointed collar, loose bodice, fairly wide rolled-up sleeves, full red skirt and the heavy apron of the rural costume.

The eighteenth century in western Europe, with one or two exceptions, saw the first real development of the rural regional costume. In England it was just the opposite; the working owners of farms, most of them hardworking and thrifty, had wives who, if they lived near the

313. BRITISH ISLES, 1808: Skye, Scotland. The trews which were worn when the kilt was forbidden. (Print Room, Victoria and Albert Museum)

314. BRITISH ISLES, 1808: Ireland. Irish Ostler. (Print Room, Victoria & Albert Museum)

315. BRITISH ISLES, 1808: Skye, Scotland. Ferryman. (Print Room, Victoria & Albert Museum)

316. BRITISH ISLES, early twentieth century: Worcestershire, England. Countryman, showing the yarks or yorks, i.e. trouser straps. *(People of all Nations)*

rapidly increasing manufacturing towns, preferred to buy their material there instead of spinning and weaving it as in former centuries. Even in remote parts of the country the countrywoman's dress became more and more a simplified imitation of the fashionable lady's dress. Peter Kalm, the Swedish visitor to rural England in 1748 remarks that "weaving and spinning in most of the houses are more than a rare thing, because their many manufacturers save them from necessity of such. Nearly all the evening occupations which our women in Sweden perform are neglected by them." This description mostly referred to the more prosperous farmers' wives; for a time the poorer rural women still continued to weave and spin their own clothes and linen, but on a smaller scale than in western Europe.

It is difficult to decide whether the Enclosures ruined the small peasant owner and cottager or whether, because the landlord had more money to develop the land more scientifically, they were a benefit to England, even at the expense of the cottager. Arthur Young, the writer on agricultural matters in the eighteenth century, was entirely in agreement with the latter theory, and his ideas are supported by Traill and Mann in their nineteenth-century social history.

E. W. Martin, author of *The Secret People* and an authority on village life, takes the opposite view. W. G. Hoskins in *The Midland Peasant* shows very clearly that his Leicestershire village would have been reduced to poverty if the stocking industry had not been accepted and developed there. Of course many small home industries helped the cottager, but, whatever the economic gain or loss, the agricultural revolution and the loss of their homes drove the poorer rural people into the industrial towns from which they never returned, and those who remained became the hired labourers of the big houses and the prosperous farmers. The result was that the English rural people gradually lost their status of small peasant owners with a highly concentrated but remote life, as was normal in the farming countries of Europe. Therefore there was no urge to develop an individual costume and the prosperous farmer's wife or daughter preferred to be as fashionable as she could. The French Revolution, with the repeal of the Sumptuary Laws on costume which gave such an impetus to European costume did not affect England, as the laws in England had been abolished in 1612[1] leaving people to wear what they liked.

There were two distinctive rural garments in England in the eighteenth and nineteenth centuries – the scarlet cloak and the sun-bonnet, but these were general, not regional. One of the earliest of the eighteenth-century rural engravings shows a dairymaid wearing the long basqued jacket with a back centre seam, a narrow rolled collar, sleeves to the elbow, with under-sleeves, a full and rather short skirt with the bands

1. *See* Appendix I on The Sumptuary Laws.

317. BRITISH ISLES, eighth century: England. (Strutt)   318. BRITISH ISLES, eighth century: England. (Strutt)
319. NORWAY, nineteenth century. (Lexow)   320. DENMARK, seventeenth century in origin: Amager.
(Mygdal)   321. DENMARK, seventeenth century in origin: Amager. (Mygdal)   322. SPAIN, 1529.
Water-carrier. (Weiditz)   323. GERMANY, twentieth century: Marburg.   324. DENMARK, seventeenth
century in origin: Amager   325. BRITISH ISLES, 1808: Scotland   326. FRANCE, 1731. (Cochin)
327. DENMARK, 1807. (Lexow)   328. DENMARK, 1807. (Lexow)   329. DENMARK, seventeenth century:
Amager. Mourning cap, white linen. (Ellen Andersen)   330. DENMARK, seventeenth century: Amager.
(Ellen Andersen)   331. DENMARK, seventeenth century: Amager. Cross cloth or forehead cloth; a square
folded diagonally under cap. (Ellen Andersen)   332. DENMARK, seventeenth century: Amager. Band of
linen to keep hair in place under cap. (Ellen Andersen)   333. DENMARK, seventeenth century: Amager.
(Ellen Andersen)   334. DENMARK, seventeenth century: Amager. (Ellen Andersen)

so much worn in rural costume, a plain apron and a tight-fitting cap, leather shoes with thick soles and low heels. This type of dress probably continued to be worn for some time. By the middle of the eighteenth century the long or short basqued bodice shows a more definite fashionable influence. The bodice part was smarter, the back had two side seams as well as a centre one, which made it a better fit. Actually this way of cutting a bodice is seen in *Le Livre des Saisons* a French illuminated book of the early sixteenth century. It reappeared in the fashionable eighteenth-century dress. A kerchief was worn, folded triangularly with a deep point at the back and two ends hanging in front, but it was also sometimes worn fichu-wise folded across the bodice and tied behind. Another way was to wear it tucked into the bodice in front. The ruffs and flat falling collars of the sixteenth and seventeenth centuries had quite disappeared. Occasionally the corset-bodice was laced in front, and very occasionally behind. Sleeves were usually to the elbow with a turned-back cuff. When the long basque was worn it often gave a pannier-like effect. In a Douce collection print of 1759 a girl hop-worker, wears a straight basqued corset-bodice, laced behind, with a sleeved smock or shift showing above it. Aprons were on the whole longer and fuller and sometimes met at the back. Coifs enclosed the hair either with a full crown and a wide frill ending in points either side of the face, or were small and tight-fitting with a narrow band; also a mob cap with a narrow pleated frill was worn. The coifs or caps had not the variety of the continental headgear, but S. Grimm's numerous drawings of small figures in his architectural surveys of the last quarter of the eighteenth century do show a certain variety, although nothing regional; with the coif was worn the straw hat with a low crown and brim curved towards the face. The hooded cloak was much used, mostly by older women, but it became more general in the early nineteenth century. Sometimes it was black or green, but usually it was red.

Peter Kalm, on a visit to a farmer's family, writes: "The women all go laced and use for every day a sort of manteau (probably the long basqued jacket) made commonly of brownish camelot. The headgear the same as London (the tight or frilled cap). It is not unusual to see a farmer's or another small personage's wife on Sundays like a lady of quality and her every day attire in proportion. Panniers are seldom used in the country. When they go out they always wear straw hats, wheat straw pretty enough. On high they wear ruffles." This is interesting as I have never seen an eighteenth century rural painting or print showing ruffles. Kalm probably meant the draped kerchief or fichu.

The costumes described above were probably those worn by the more prosperous farming community. The poorer rural women wore also the short or long basqued bodice, mostly hooked. In the early

335. FRANCE, 1416 *(Les Très Riches Heures du Duc de Berry)*   336. ITALY, 1412. *(L'Ufiziolo Visconteo)*
337. FLANDERS, 1568. (Breughel)   338. BELGIUM, 1830 (Madou)   339. BRITISH ISLES, late fifteenth century:
England. (Strutt)   340. NORWAY, c. 1300: Bergen. (From a mural)   341. FLANDERS, 1565. (Breughel)
342. FLANDERS, 1565. (Breughel)   343. FLANDERS, 1565. (Breughel)   344. FLANDERS, 1565. (Breughel)
345. AUSTRIA, nineteenth century: Vorarlberg. (Helm)   346. GERMANY, 1580. (Amman)   347. GERMANY,
nineteenth century: Bavaria. (Helm)

nineteenth century the basque became much longer. In the north of England a draped handkerchief was worn over the head and round the neck, and topping this a square-crowned felt hat, the effect being very early seventeenth-century.

A Wensleydale woman wears a high crowned hat with a narrow brim, a Durham woman in Grimm's drawings (1790) has a curiously shaped peaked black hood-like hat, and another, burning kelpie, has a crochet coif with strings. The dresses vary very little, but the headgear continues to do so.

The shoes of the prosperous rural woman were leather with buckles of steel, silver or metal. Buckled shoes were worn even when milking, but the rougher type of women wore heavy mannish shoes with very thick soles. Pattens were worn out of doors, and were still worn in the early part of the twentieth century. Clogs were worn in the North, but English rural women never wore the continental sabot, and there are no drawings in Grimm showing barefooted countrywomen as in Scotland and Ireland.

George Walker has many paintings in his book of Yorkshire costume and there is a good deal of variety in the dresses. The "Rowkers" wore a sort of buttoned man's coat for rough work, had scarves draped over their coifs as a protection against the sun, and many girls had a sort of straw poke-bonnet.

The dress of the Filey fisher-girl has a distinctly regional look, with apparently a tight corset-bodice, with a long basque, a fine pointed kerchief, short skirt and an interesting European-looking coif, with a full crown gathered into a narrow band and a winged front piece framing the face. She is shown with bare legs and feet like European fisher-girls.

A painting by Bristow in 1822 shows an elderly countrywoman still wearing the eighteenth-century kerchief and bodice, though by now the sleeves have the fullness of the early nineteenth century. She still has a frilled white coif, such as was worn by an elderly carol singer in Herefordshire in the last quarter of the nineteenth century. A Herefordshire spinner also wore a tight-fitting coif with the long floating ends of a much earlier period. Neither of these coifs resembles the elaborate creations worn by the middle-class women of this period. She also wore the heavy wide white cotton apron.

There is a description in Ella Mary Leather's book *Folk Lore of Hereford* of the dress, circa 1860, of old Martha B——: "Her dress was linsey woolsey. Beneath the cotton coif, which will soon be obsolete, she wore an old-fashioned black cap, with ribbon and lace frilling covering the ears, while her woolled crossover and her wide apron were so often as not worn wrong side out."

348. GERMANY, 1580. (Amman)   349. GERMANY, 1570. (Dürer)   350. DENMARK, nineteenth century.
(Ellen Andersen)   351. SWITZERLAND, c. 1835. (Hierli)   352. GERMANY, 1570. (Dürer)   353. ITALY,
fourteenth century. (*Tacuinum Sanitatis*)   354. SPAIN, 1529. Basque. (Weiditz)   355. BRITISH ISLES, early
twentieth century: Connemara, Ireland. Red flannel petticoat over head like a cloak. (*People of all
Nations*)   356. GERMANY, Marburg. (Helm)   357. GERMANY, 1520. (Dürer)   358. FRANCE, Gouëzec,
Brittany. (From a photograph)   359. GERMANY, twentieth century: Lindhorst. (Helm)   360. GERMANY,
twentieth century: Lindhorst. (Helm)   361. FRANCE, Pont L'Abbé. (From a photograph)

In 1850, in a Hereford pamphlet, the writer says: "a farmer must buy his wife a Paris cap, bonnet, hat or dress or any kind of French millinery." Up to the First World War the sun-bonnet was worn out of doors and had replaced the coif or cap.

The plain straw poke-bonnet trimmed with a pale blue ribbon was very much a rural fashion in the middle of the century; black straw ones were also worn, and both are frequently seen in the paintings of this period. Mrs. Woolf of Barns Green, aged 98 years, who lived on the estate of the Bruces of Brundell, remembers the village children wearing straw bonnets and scarlet cloaks.

When the scarlet cloak, the straw bonnet, the sunbonnet and the big white apron disappeared at the end of the nineteenth century, every vestige of rural costume disappeared with them, and country- and townswomen dressed alike according to their taste and means.

Ireland

Irish dress has a special place in the history of rural costume. It is the one national costume worn by the majority of the people which was forbidden by law for political reasons.

The Sumptuary Laws which were made to destroy this dress dealt particularly with the Irish mantle, the *leine* or *tunica*, the trews or trousers and the saffron-yellow colour which was much used by the Irish. These laws forbade men to wear their hair long and prohibited the characteristic Irish embroideries. Details of these laws will be found in the chapter on Sumptuary Laws on costume.

The Irish mantle, the *leine* and trews all date from a very early period and were worn long after these garments had been discarded in the rest of western Europe, though the long *leine* or tunic survives in the shirt or tunic of the Berbers, Arabs and Egyptians.

A very characteristic garment of the Irish was their mantle. One of the earliest records of this garment is in the writings of Giraldus Cambrensis (1186)[1], and one of his editors, Thomas Wright, says: "Their custom is to wear small close fitting hoods hanging below the shoulders a cubits length, generally made of parti-coloured strips sewn together; under these they use woollen rugs instead of cloaks."

Thomas Wright, in 1892, says that what Cambrensis calls *caputum* was a sort of bonnet and hood protecting not only the head, but the neck and shoulders also. It was of conical form probably made of the same stuff as the mantle, to describe which Cambrensis used the Latin word *phalingum* (Irish, *falad*) which signifies a rug or covering of

1. Giraldus Cambrensis, translated by Sir R. Colt Hoare.

362. FLANDERS, 1565. (Breughel)   363. SPAIN, 1529: Valencia. (Weiditz)   364. GERMANY, twentieth century: Black Forest. Pompons, red for unmarried girls, black for married women. 365. GERMANY, nineteenth century: Kleines Walsertal.   366. SWITZERLAND, 1829. (Hierli)   367. BRITISH ISLES, twentieth century: Wales   368. BRITISH ISLES, nineteenth century: England   369. BRITISH, ISLES, 1623-24   370. U.S.A., nineteenth century. Quilted gingham bonnet, brown and white   371. BRITISH ISLES, mid-nineteenth century: England   372. BELGIUM, first half nineteenth century. Milk girl from district of Antwerp

any sort. This cloak had a fringed border sewn or woven down the edges. It was worn almost as low as the ankles, and was usually made of frieze or some such coarse material. It was also worn by the higher classes in the same fashion but was made of better material.

The hooded cape was common to most rural people at this period. Cunnington says of the brat of the ninth and tenth century that it was a short coarse mantle worn by peasantry, a humble imitation of the *Saga Tressonica*.[1] H. F. McClintock calls it a brat, and says it was pre-Norman. It was known also as the Cochull brat or hooded cloak.

It is, however, the blanket or ruggy or fringed cloak – Norse-Celtic mantle – which is the interesting garment and this was forbidden by English Sumptuary Laws. This fringed mantle was worn by the Irish. It is seen in many contemporary sixteen-century illustrations. A full description of this mantle will be found in chapter II.

The garment is typically Celtic, as are the trews or trousers, which Cambrensis described as covering the lower part of the thigh and legs with hose and stockings made in one or sewn to them. His editor remarks: "A garment common to the Celtic nation and often mentioned by Roman writers – one of the provinces of Gaul had the name of Gallia Braccata for these trews. They were often parti-coloured and were similar to those of the Scots. The name trews originates from the French *Trebus* and, before 1200, *Tross*."

McClintock[2] says that in pre-Norman days men wore the brat and *leine*, jacket and trews and that both costumes were worn until the sixteenth century and, amalgamated, survived to form a composite costume which included the brat, jacket, *leine* and trews all in one.

The leine, the third important early Irish garment, is like a long Greek *chiton* or a Roman *tunica*. In a sixteenth-century illustration it has an embroidered top overlay with thigh-length pleats – making this garment different from all other forms of rural tunics.

Derrick, in the sixteenth century, writes:

> *Their skirts be very strange*
> *Not reaching past the thigh*
> *With pleats on pleats they pleated*
> *Whose sleeves hang trailing down*
> *Almost unto the shoe.*

This garment when shown in illustrations is often trimmed with fringes, has no trews to it, but is partially covered by the mantle sometimes worn over the head.

The "Wild Irish", as the English called the poorer Irish country people, had a simple *leine* or tunic under their fringed mantle like the

1. C. W. Cunnington, *Handbook of English Medieval Costume.*
2. H. F. McClintock, *Old Irish and Highland Dress*, 1943.

373. GERMANY   374. GERMANY, Buckeburg. *(People of all Nations)*   375. NORWAY   376 GERMANY
377. GERMANY, Sankt Georgien. Myriad-coloured glass balls. *(People of All Nations)*   378. GERMANY

Welsh. The men wore the more elaborate *leine* – and later, in the sixteenth century, a simple form – were bare-legged and without shoes, and have the long shaggy hair forbidden by the Sumptuary Laws.

Rural women in the early days probably wore a long tunic covered by a full fringed mantle. The "Wild Irishwoman" is shown wearing such a mantle; under it she is wearing either a very short tunic or nothing at all. She is bare-legged and shoeless. The colour of the shirts is like saffron yellow, which, probably extracted from various lichens, was easily obtainable. The saffron dye was too expensive for general use.

When the Sumptuary Laws began to have their effect at the end of the sixteenth century, the Irish costume became more anglicised, as the makers of the laws intended that it should. In McClintock's excellent and scholarly book there is an illustration of an Irish House Boy and a Kerne in 1581. Instead of the long *leine* they wear an adaptation of the sixteenth-century jerkin with a full basque; only the neck-opening, formed by a long rolled collar, is much wider and deeper than the English type, and the wide, open and medieval sleeves are Irish. Both men apparently have long-sleeved vests under the jerkins. The house boy has bare legs and feet, but his hair is cut in the English fashion. The Kerne's hair is Irish and shaggy, but he has trews and heel-less square-toed shoes. According to Walker, the tight trews woven in strips or divisions (checks) were worn by peasants in the seventeenth century. McClintock says breeches, called trews, of white frieze were worn in 1644. In 1630 the trews had a pouch in front and were drawn together by a string. The jerkin with a skirted basque with side and back slits was worn in the early seventeenth century. It was made of coarse linen or hemp and, according to McClintock, a frieze coat was worn over it in the winter. There seems to be no record of the men's dress of the later seventeenth or early eighteenth century, but the rural people probably came under the influence of the English settlers. In the more remote hilly district the main garment of the poor Irish was probably the mantle and the belted plaid, of coarse local weave and dyed with local dyes. It served in the remote Welsh districts as both blanket and cloak.

The rural women in the sixteenth and early seventeenth centuries continued to wear the fringed cloak, and when they could not afford this, wrapped themselves in a white sheet. No skirts were worn with the mantle.

In northern Ireland the women wore the mantle or rug doubled and belted round the body and fastened at the neck (belted plaid). Evidently the Sumptuary Laws had not entirely killed the Irish dress in the early seventeenth century. Joseph Walker in the eighteenth century gives a rare detailed description of an Irishwoman's dress in the second half of the seventeenth century. The dress was worn by a Mary Morgan, who was married before the Boyne, and the details of it were handed down. The description is interesting because it is of a very traditional western European rural costume: "Jacket was of brown cloth or pressed frieze to fit close and shaped by means of whale bone brought into the jacket before and behind, and this was laced in front and not as to meet and through the lacing was drawn the ends of the neck kerchief. The sleeves came half way to the elbow, were made of the same kind of cloth as the jacket, then continued to the wrist of red chamlet stripped with green ferreting and these being turned up formed a little cuff embroidered with three circles of green riband. (These were probably the separate sleeves used so much in the Welsh and European rural costumes.) Her Petticoat (skirt) either of scarlet frieze or cloth, bordered with three rows of green riband (a very traditional rural detail). Her apron of green serge striped lengthways, blue hose and black leather shoes." The description of Mary Morgan's head-dress is most interesting. She wore "a roll of linen on her head (a survival of the better-to-do Irish woman and forbidden by the sixteenth-century Sumptuary Laws) like those on which milk maids carry their pails, higher behind than before with a little round-eared cap or coif with border sewed on plain, over this was thrown a kerchief which in her youth was made fast on the top of the head and let fall carelessly behind – in her old age it was pinned under the chin." (This kerchief tied under the chin can be seen in many of the Welsh eighteenth-century dresses.) Walker mentions her shoes, called brogues in the sixteenth century, and McClintock gives 1644 as a date when they were worn. They were single-soled shoes more roughly sewn than is usual in a shoe, sharp at the toes and with a flap of leather at the heel to pull them on, but both writers think the poorer Irish went barefooted.

In Wheatley's painting of an Irish Fair in 1783 the men wear a knee-length full and shapeless coat with a big collar and cuffs, with two big buttons on the back seams. Some of these coats were blue and brown, but some were the natural off-white of the traditional frieze, the same as that which the men of Galway wore into the present century. It is also the colour of the natural Welsh flannel, a strong wiry material probably used in Ireland. The men wore high-crowned felt hats with wide floppy brims, and also three-cornered hats, and later probably some bourgeois cast-off breeches and blue and white striped stockings, and heavy leather shoes completed the dress. One of the women in the picture is wrapped in a brown cloak with a deep collar, yellow skirt and floppy felt hat over a white coif.

All these dresses are completely anglicised. One woman, however, is wearing a short hooded cloak more like the descendant of the short brat than the normally long rural cloak with a hooded collar.

In Galway until quite lately the women wore heavy red skirts dyed with local madder, and printed woollen shawls.

In the Irish volume of *People of All Nations* published about 1922, there is a photograph of a woman in a long blue hooded cloak, called the Irish cloak. This cloak is still worn in Kinsale, County Cork, but is known as the Munster cloak. It is of fine black cloth and when the hood is drawn over the head the effect is quite medieval.

Scotland

The costume associated with Scotland is obviously the tartan and kilt, but that was confined to certain districts of the country. It was not a peasant dress, though it was one of the few examples in western Europe of a definitely national costume. Originally, the "ployde" or plaid always associated with the kilt was most likely the main, possibly the sole, garment of the poorer people, and in this resembled the Irish and Welsh rug-mantles.

Stuart Maxwell, in his book *Scottish Costume*, writes: "The plaid was five ells double width woollen material, not necessarily tartan, and for wet and cold draped over the head and shoulders, and when not in use over one shoulder and tied bandolier fashion." For the Lowlander, this was an outdoor garment.

The other characteristic garment for poorer people was the tam o'shanter, mostly worn flat on the head. It certainly dates from the sixteenth century. McClintock[1] gives a 1743 illustration of a belted plaid in his book; this is worn slung from the shoulders, belted and folded over in front, forming deep hanging sleeves and is more enveloping than the Irish mantle. With this plaid was worn a vest-like garment, with a slit in front, like the Irish sixteenth-century vest. Tartan hose to above the knee with ties and high shoes, flat bonnet with a bow at the back and longish hair complete the costume.

Most likely the women in early times wore the plaid as mantle; according to Stuart Maxwell, in the sixteenth century they veiled their faces when out of doors, leaving only one eye visible, which seems to link this garment with that ancient mantle the *huik*, which originated from north Africa and which had an influence on so many European rural mantles. Of all the costumes of the British Isles the early Scottish rural dress is most scantily recorded all through the centuries. What there is is difficult to trace, and yet this is the only country of the British Isles in which a regional dress developed and still exists.

1. H. F. McClintock, *Old Irish and Highland Dress*, 1943.

As the records of the costume are few, one can only fall back on deduction and comparison. For instance, Thomas Kirke in his journey through Scotland in 1679 records that the poorer people in the lowlands "go almost naked, only for a cloak, a part of their bedclothes thrown over them". This "bedcloth" was probably the blanket-like garment used in Wales and part of the West Country, called the whittle. The country people living nearer the towns in the Lowlands would be better dressed, because since the Middle Ages, the Scottish Royal Boroughs promoted a big trade in wool, first to Flanders, and later to the Dutch Island of Walcheren, and by the seventeenth century "kersies", a coarse narrow woollen cloth, were included in their exports. That the rural people of the Lowlands adopted the same simple dress as was worn across the border is shown in the engraving from Grant's *Everyday Life in Scotland*[1]. A shepherd is seen wearing a summer, belted tunic-frock with a deep rolled collar, and breeches or hose resembling the old Gaulish trews with dagged edges. The hose have a hole deliberately cut in the knee, which is often found amongst the poorer peasants of western Europe, especially shepherds. The lower part of the legs and feet are bare. A high oval-crowned hat with brim, pulled well down over the head for shade, and a side pouch, complete the dress. The winter dress has knee-high boots, hat with upturned brim and sporting a bird's feather; a plaid was probably worn over the tunic frock.

The women in early times would have worn a coarse woollen gown, woven and dyed locally, and probably somewhat shorter than the medieval English rural gown. The most interesting record is a mid-seventeenth-century picture by G. Witt called *The Highland Dance*. This is the most important painting relating to Scottish rural costume I have yet found, especially as it concerns the seventeenth century of which there are so few rural records. Also, it is the only pictorial confirmation of a custom often recorded, that clothing, either new or cast off, was given in lieu of wages. The central dancing figure of a girl wears the pointed boned bodice with a low almost horizontal wide opening, very short sleeves and fastened behind. It seems to be of velvet and is the apparel of a fashionable lady. (There are several photographs of this type of bodice in the Victoria and Albert Museum.) It was certainly given or lent to the dancer for a special occasion. The rest of her costume is rural: a simple long skirt to the ankles, light in colour; a long, full yet narrow apron; stockings and pointed shoes tied with thongs. Her smock has full elbow-sleeves ending in a frill. On her head she wears the typical seventeenth-century kerchief tied under the chin, over that a rather shapeless coif. A kneeling woman wears the usual rural low-cut hooked bodice with elbow-sleeves and her smock sleeves are visible. Two other women are wrapped in Highland plaids, one with her head

1. Part I.

enveloped, the other, bareheaded, with long floating hair, wears a plain skirt and apron.

The men's costumes are even more heterogeneous. The chief dancer is trimmed with ribbon. This dancer wears a long and fairly full-skirted coat of the period, knee breeches, long hose and heeled shoes. The sleeves of his coat reach to below the elbow and his shirt with a narrow turn-down collar has sleeves that protrude from the coat sleeves and reach to the wrist.

One man is draped in a voluminous tartan plaid which reaches to his feet, but does not cover his head; another figure has tartan trews. Two other men wear a non-Highland dress, with the flat falling collar of the period, and a loose coat to just below the knee of the *casaque* pattern, the other a loose cloak resembling those worn by the French painter le Nain's rural figures. The most interesting of all the men is a "gallant" rustic; he also wears a laird's discarded jerkin of an earlier period, to just below the waist, with slashed sleeves from which emerge his shirt sleeves. He has breeches tied at the knee, stockings, and fairly pointed black shoes. From his jerkin protrudes a pouch and sheathed knife. Under the flat bonnets the men's hair is straight and shoulder-length.

Scottish women prided themselves on walking barefoot and only wore shoes for church, either double- or single-soled, though earlier on leather shoes were more universal. The laced corset-bodice of the warmer countries never seems to have been worn in Scotland. The traditional rural narrow and long apron was worn. J. Brome in his *Travels in England, Scotland and Wales* (1700) says: "The country people agree with the Wild Irish. They go habited in Mantles of striped or streaked with colours about their shoulders which they call Bodies, and commonly naked upon their legs, but wear sandals upon the soles of their feet. The women go clad much after the same fashion."

By the end of the eighteenth century the rural inhabitants of the Isles of Skye were wearing much the same dress as country people in the north of England. There are some interesting water colours done probably in the early part of the nineteenth century of named local people over the age of 80 years[1]. One woman wears a characteristic fishwife's dress: a black and mauvy-pink striped heavy wool skirt resembling the material and colouring of the late eighteenth-century Welsh *betgwyn*, a yellow and striped waistcoat, a dark blue and reddy-pink check shawl-like mantle lined with black, a typical seventeenth-century kerchief folded over the head and crossed round the neck in front and an unusual hat of cloth, royal blue and with a reddish pink check, turned down at the back and turned up high in front. On her back she carries a big fish basket secured by a strap passing over the front shoulders. She has bare feet.

1. Victoria and Albert Museum. Print Department.

Mrs. McDougal wears the dress of a farmer's wife: a heavy black skirt, a black loose corsage with full deep basque, three-quarter length sleeves, deep turned-back cuffs. A dark and light-blue checked kerchief is worn over the corsage and crossed in front. The apron is blue and white striped, long and narrow of the eighteenth-century type. A white mob-like coif with a frill passing under the chin and a ribbon band over the forehead. Her shoes are heavy and black with low heels. Murdoch Gilles' "Ferryman" has long brown trousers, and buttoned waistcoat, black coat and knotted kerchief over the shirt: a southern-type dress, except that the crown of the black, brimmed hat is higher and goes to a point on top; and heavy shoes with low heels are worn.

More characteristic Scottish details appear in the dress of another old man (Archibald Maxwell): trousers or trews of green and yellow tartan, a hip-length coat of blackberry red and blue striped cloth (a Welsh-like material). His waistcoat is mustard yellow cloth with a double row of buttons and deep revers; a floppy black hat with high flat crown and a light ribbon; black and white striped socks and low single-soled heel-less shoes.

Allan Ramsay shows a Scottish spinning woman in 1788 with a hooked bodice, long sleeves, full skirt and an unusual tartan apron with a deep fringe. She has a hooded cap with a shoulder-length frill.

Countrywomen of this period also wore the lustrous red country cloak called the Cardinal cloak, and the farmers sometimes wore a black bonnet as opposed to the blue bonnets of the farm workers[1].

Ivor Brown in *Balmoral* quotes from *A Stag Party* by John Taylor (1815): "Their habit is shoes made with one sole a piece, stockings which they call short hose, made of a warm stuff of divers colours, which they call tartans, breeches, many of them or their forefathers never wore any – a jerkin of the same stuff as their hose. Gaiters being bands or weaths of straw or hay – a plaid about their shoulders of divers colours of a finer length of stuff than their hose, blue flat caps on their heads. Handkerchiefs, knotted with two knots about their neck."

This had probably been their costume for at least a hundred years, except the fashionable addition of the late eighteenth century, a knotted kerchief.

In John Kay's *Series of English Portraits* (1838)[2] there are descriptions of fishwives' dresses of Newhaven, Fisherrow and Dunbar: as these places are the only ones mentioned as having a special dress, they were obviously of unusual interest, even in the early nineteenth century. Kay says "Newhaven's exclusive intercourse has distinguished them from time immemorial and that Newhaven Fishermen Benefit Society was instituted by charter James VI". Newhaven and Fisherrow are now

1. Stuart Maxwell, *Scottish Costume*.
2. John Kay's *Series of English Portraits (Scotland)* 1838. Notes by Hugh Paton.

part of Edinburgh. Paton[1] also mentions that "Buckhaven fishermen on the opposite coast are said to be descendants from Netherlanders and wore the wide trousers and long boots of the Dutch, but there are no positive grounds for thinking that fishers of Prestonpans, Fisherrow or Newhaven derive from such stock."

However, it is quite possible that refugees in the sixteenth century, persecuted by the Spaniards for their Calvinistic faith, fled to the Scottish coast, for at that time Scotland had a big wool trading centre on the island of Walcheren, where the long, wide trousers were worn by seafaring men; but as no study appears to have been made on this subject it is impossible to make more than a surmise.

The Newhaven fishwife's dress, as shown in early twentieth-century photographs, has a continental look, but it is obviously eighteenth-century in derivation, and somewhat resembles the Welsh dress. There is nothing Dutch in origin about the Newhaven dress in these photographs or in the 1838 engravings. However, the front turn-up of the top skirt is the same as that of Belgian rural women of the early nineteenth century; these women also carried heavy baskets strapped on their backs. What makes the Newhaven and Fisherrow dress exceptional is that the strap of the basket passes across the forehead, instead of over the chest, as is the usual way.

That this dress is still in existence makes it quite unique in the British Isles. It probably owes its survival to the fact that fisher people in most parts of the world have lived in isolated communities, and have therefore retained costumes and customs that even the conservative rural people have lost through contact with manufacturing and industrial centres.

As this dress is so unusual I will give in full the description by Hugh Paton in John Kay's *Portraits*: "A cap of cotton or linen surmounted by stout napkin tied below the chin, composes the investiture of the head, the more showy construction wherewith other females are adorned being inadmissable. From the broad belt crossing the forehead supported the creel (that is the fish basket), a sort of pea jacket of vast amplitude of skirt conceals upper part of the person relieved at the throat by an ample display of handkerchief. The under part of the figure is invested with voluminous quantities of petticoats of substantial material and gaudy colour generally yellow with stripes."

Stuart Maxwell quotes Mitchell, who said in 1780: "Countrywomen's dress is strong and serviceable, mainly drugget, a striped woollen cloth locally woven", and goes on to say that this survives in the Newhaven dress.

Paton says: "These skirts gave a very free inspection of the ankle and were worn in such immense number as the bare mention of them

1. John Kay's *Series of English Portraits (Scotland)*, 1838. Notes by Hugh Paton.

would make a lady faint. One half of these ample garments is gathered up over the haunches, puffing out the figure in an unusual and uncouth way." (This wearing of several petticoats was common in many European countries, especially in Holland, until the end of the nineteenth century.) White worsted stockings and stout shoes completed this costume.

Paton ends this description by saying that the fishwives have a slight stoop forward, a firm and elastic step, a slight turn of toes inwards. They had ruddy complexions, and three of them went in 1795 from Dunbar to Edinburgh, 27 miles, with 200 lbs of herring on their backs in five hours. They sometimes even carried 250 lbs.

The dresses in Kay's engraved portraits vary; one woman has a long-sleeved jacket with a deep basque with a back slit; another just has a long-sleeved bodice; both are of plain material; a checked pointed kerchief, and the top striped petticoat is rolled up pannier fashion, similar to the Welsh dress. One has a striped petticoat with three bands just above the hem, stout shoes, tied, not strapped. On the head, the traditional late eighteenth-century flowered and checked kerchief, with a narrow band and tied under the chin, English and Welsh fashion. Two of the women carrying their creels in the very special way of this district with the strap of the creel across their foreheads; the third woman has hers passing over her chest in the usual way.

The Newhaven fishwife of the late nineteenth and early twentieth centuries has a dark blue and white striped underskirt, the same as in the Kay prints. The top skirt is a deep blue with a dark blue stripe and is lined with a red and white striped material. This skirt is rolled up and forms a point in front, in the fashion seen in France and Belgium in the early nineteenth century. A flowered blouse with short sleeves and white turned-back cuffs is tucked into the skirt and blue ribbon tied in front with long ends encircling the waist. The hair is brushed back and is covered with a fringed and coloured scarf, which replaces the old kerchief.

A black early nineteenth-century type cloak hangs almost to the hem of the skirt. Ordinary shoes and stockings are worn. The fish-wife's hands rest on a large fish creel placed next to her.

Mr. Stuart Maxwell, of the National Museum of Antiquities of Scotland, has kindly sent me a list of the present-day garment, with details of the Fisherrow woman's dress, of which I will give the principal points:

DAY COSTUME
Flowered blouse of pink satin.

Waistcoat of navy blue wool.

Skirt of green, blue and brown fine tweed. Apron of navy blue and white striped material.

Coat of navy blue wool with high standing collar.

Shawl of black and white check wool.

Thick black laced shoes, but stretch nylon stockings in place of the hand-knitted woollen ones formerly worn.

GALA DRESS

Blouse of blue printed flowered spun rayon.

Square turned collar, sleeves wide and straight having white cotton turned back cuffs.

Underskirt of navy blue and cream striped wool, with a basque of cream linen, overskirt of red and white striped wool pleated to a basque of white linen.

Apron of narrow blue and white striped cotton gathered into a broad waistband.

Shawl of cream wool printed with sprays of flowers and leaves.

Black silk stockings, black leather shoes with decorated flap.

Pocket of spun rayon.

Mr. Maxwell was kind enough to write that the Fisherrow fishwife calls once a week at his home, and up to the end of August 1959 carried her creel on her back with the strap across her forehead in the "old way", and she still had the forward bend to her head. Now the fish will be carried in a mechanised arrangement like a golfer's caddy. It is to be hoped that the rest of this unique Scottish rural costume will remain unaltered for many years to come.

Wales

The Welsh dress is probably the best example of a rural fashion that developed regional characteristics in the eighteenth century which became more pronounced in the nineteenth century and only disappeared from *daily* use in 1890. The costumes are still sometimes worn for special occasions.

Even the popular picture postcard has done something to preserve the memory of this interesting costume.

The Welsh dress is also a good example of how regional characteristics were confined well within their own country, though an exception to this is the mass emigration of farming people to another country, for example the sixteenth-century Dutch from West Friesland to Denmark, where they continued to wear their own dress until it disappeared in the nineteenth century.

Though the regional costume of border provinces was apt to be influenced by the countries on either side, the rural costume as a rule did not migrate: this was the big difference between fashionable and rural dress. This does not mean that the basic rural garments of various countries differed greatly: all western European dress has a basic resemblance. The costume of Wales belongs basically to Europe and, as in Europe, it developed a distinctive peasant dress, which England never did. The reason for this dissimilarity between the two lands was the geographical isolation of Wales with its wild countryside, rugged hills and mountains and its difficult land approaches on the one hand and the sea on the other. It was, however, not industrially isolated, owing to the quantities of sheep and their wool, which certainly gave work to a large number of cottage weavers. Proximity to numerous streams also gave rise to many small family mills in various parts of the country, where the wiry, rough but very hard-wearing wool was turned into a coarse material. From the eighteenth century onwards the mills employed local labour. What they produced was available to the local inhabitants, and as water played a big role where non-chemical dyes were used, this probably accounted for the great variety of colours in the materials.

The so-called Flemish influence in Welsh costume is one of those legends which originated in a remark by Pyne in his *Welsh Dress* (1824): "The character of the whole is much in the character of the Flemish peasantry." A later writer ascribes it to the Flemish weavers who settled in Pembrokeshire.

These people, according to Dr. B. G. Charles in *Non-Celtic Place Names in Wales,* were planted in 1107 by Henry I in the centre of Ros (now Roose) in Pembrokeshire. Geraldus Cambrensis, the Welsh chronicler of the twelfth century, describes this alien population as brave, hardy and hostile to the Welsh industries; they were agriculturists, merchants and weavers. These Flemings were quickly anglicised through contact with England before and after their migration.

The Flemings probably left their country owing to early small wars and local disturbances and were attracted by the raw materials of the British Isles. They were woollen weavers, but they also had great skill in the making of fine linen and damask, for which Flanders was renowned in medieval times. It is out of the question that twelfth-century weavers, whose men and women wore the short and long cote or tunic, a very simple garment, could have influenced the costume of the eighteenth- and nineteenth-century Welsh farmers' wives. The garment Pyne refers to is the *betgwyn* or bedgown – *jaquette* or jacket – which had a basic eighteenth-century cut influenced by the sixteenth-century women's *jaquette* of France and other western European countries.

It is strange and sad that the Welsh dress, which has such a special place in the history of British rural costume, has practically no traceable history before the eighteenth century. The records of the Irish and even the Highland dress, scanty though they are, tell us more about their origin than anything anyone has so far found out about the Welsh.

The probability is that the blanket cloak was the main garment of the rural people and, like the Irish and Highlanders, they wore it day and night. Sheepskin was used, with the wool worn inside for cloaks and outside for "high shoes" – probably these were the main garments worn by shepherds. The women wove the wool of their wiry sheep into a harsh, springy but indestructible material, the ancestor of the famous Welsh flannel.

Giraldus Cambrensis writes: "Their dress at night differs not from the day. They defend themselves from the cold only by a cloak and an undergarment." The latter was probably a tunic, the *leine* of the Irish. He continues: "The men and women cut their hair close round their ears and eyes. The women after the manner of the Parthians, cover their heads with a large white veil folded like a turban." He adds, "they clean their teeth with green hazel and a woollen cloth. Men shave all beards except the moustache. The legs are bare with high shoes." Another early writer speaks of a cloak and vest as the sole garments.

In the *Popular Antiquities of Wales* (1815) there is a reproduction of a twelfth-century carved seat-end from Malvern church. The figure is a peasant threshing with a hook. He wears a belted tunic with a pouch suspended from a shoulder strap. A scarf head-dress is tied behind and covers the neck, and is exactly like those worn by the Italian peasants of the same period. The footwear is unusual, a kind of Roman sandal. If the carving was local work, one can take it that this was, for some considerable time, the costume of the Welsh as well as of the English border people. The brat, the hooded short cloak, was most likely worn in winter by the border people, as it was in England and in the less remote parts of Ireland.

In 1939 Miss Megan Ellis, of the National Library of Wales, published a most valuable document listing the clothing of a servant maid employed by well-to-do country people in probably about the end of the sixteenth century. The description of the clothes, their materials and their colours add greatly to our knowledge. The maid, a country girl, often had her clothing in lieu of wages and the garments recorded over a number of years were a simpler form of those worn by her mistress, as was usually the case in England and western Europe until the end of the last quarter of the eighteenth century. The girl's clothes showed much variety both in garments and materials, and were certainly not restricted to bare necessities.

Ellen, the serving maid of Iewan Ap Rees ap David, wore a petticoat – in this case another name for what we would call a skirt – and as the making of two petticoats is noted, there was most likely an underskirt and on one occasion "white linnen" for making it is mentioned. She wore a "body", and, judging by the cut and line of the eighteenth-century *betgwyn* which much resembles the late fifteenth- and sixteenth-century French *jaquette*, this was a closed hooked corsage cut fairly low and filled in with the partlet of linen or cloth, varying probably according to the season of the year. Linen was used for a ruff and for a smock (shift?).

Black cloth is listed for an appron (apron): this is interesting because black, and black and white, were often the colours of the nineteenth-century Welsh aprons.

A woollen or flannel jerkin is mentioned: this may have been a closed jacket with a kerchief tucked in the front and worn outside at the back with a point to the waist. The tailor made the jerkin but apparently not the "body". There were also three women's "coats" which were probably the origin of the long-skirted eighteenth-century Welsh coat. A "mais" petticoat or coat (most likely the former) was worn trimmed with fringe or lace: there is a description of an English lace-trimmed rural petticoat in the seventeenth century. Linen was used for caps and felt for hats, and such luxuries as a pair of gloves, a silk girdle and little kerchiefs are listed.

Materials used for the petticoats were wool, kersey, "a coarse narrow cloth woven from wool and usually ribbed"[1] (originating from Kersey in Suffolk) and "flannen", the coarse, wiry strong Welsh flannel.

The colours most mentioned are red and *pwck* (puce). The latter is also mentioned for dyeing cloth.

Cape and kerchiefs of "linen" or "linnen cloth", "partletts of cloth and linnen", "approns" of cloth: this is certainly one of the best early records of the clothing of a well-clad working woman. In the National Library of Wales are a large number of family and estate papers waiting to be edited. Probably many more lists of personal possessions would come to light.

The laced bodice in "The Welsh Wedding" illustrated in Mr. Ken Etheridge's useful book[2] on Welsh costume is definitely an eighteenth-century bourgeois dress.

The most interesting garment of the Welsh dress is the *betgwyn* or jacket, both short- and long-skirted. It had a tight-fitting bodice, straight elbow-length sleeves and an extra sleeve from elbow to wrist, which were already worn in western Europe in the fifteenth century.

1. *New Oxford Dictionary.*
2. Ken Etheridge, *Welsh Costume* (privately printed).

As worn on the continent in the sixteenth and seventeenth centuries it always had an influence on the eighteenth-century dress; this is markedly so in Switzerland and in a minor degree in the Scandinavian countries.

The tailored back, centre and side seams of the *betgwyn* are reminiscent of earlier French rural fashions. An example of a seamless back to the bodice with its very long basque skirt, complete with partlet and ruff, as described in a serving maid's dress, can be seen in the Dutch painter Averkamp's skating scenes.

It is probably this continental influence which caused Pyne to write "A Flemish look".

The *betgwyn* followed the fashion of the earlier cherkin or jerkin and also the continental rural fashion in retaining the high-set and tight upper-sleeve and extra lower-sleeve and not adopting the fashionable low-set sleeves of the seventeenth century.

In the eighteenth century the long basque skirt of the *betgwyn* was often looped back to show the rather short, full skirts, striped, checked and plain, and over the skirt was worn a striped checked and later on a plain white apron. The partlet probably continued to be worn during the seventeenth and eighteenth centuries.

In the eighteenth century the flat straw hat with a shallow crown was worn in nearly all western European countries, including England, and was introduced into Wales prior to the tall hat, which eventually ousted it.

The famous tall hat, both in its oval and square form, also had a long history. Dutchmen in Averkamp's painting can be seen wearing it. A Brabant peasant woman in the seventeenth century wears one with a wide brim and high pointed crown (a regular witch's hat). The English country wife in 1623[1] has one with a high crown and narrow brim, and the German seventeenth-century women a square-crowned one with wide brim. These hats seem to have disappeared from fashion for a time and reappeared at the very end of the eighteenth century, when the tall hat became the fashionable headgear of the men and women of the French Directoire period and eventually the popular riding hat for women and top hat for men in most countries. It was probably from both these late sources that the well-to-do Welsh farmers' wives took their very special headgear. Mr. Ken Etheridge says there are examples marked inside with the name of a Paris firm of hat-makers.

The eighteenth- and nineteenth-century skirts (the former petticoat) were of plain or striped wool, the striped ones becoming more frequent in the latter century. The wealthier farmers' wives probably wore a quilted satin skirt; one is shown in the illustration of a Welsh market-

1. *Album Amicorum.* British Museum.

woman 1814[1]. This fashion was borrowed from the English country-woman. The colours of the plain skirts were sometimes brown and drab, many blue and green, but the striped ones were usually gay in colours.

The skirts were full and gathered in heavy folds at the waist. They had a braid finish to the hem and occasionally the very traditional band of braid or stripe of material on the lower edge of the skirt.

According to Mr. Etheridge, the colours of the skirts and petticoats varied with the district from which the wearers came, as was the case in many European countries. Many of the striped skirts resemble in colour those worn by rural and working class Frenchwomen of the eighteenth century and Dutch peasants of the nineteenth century. The skirt was often plain and was worn short to show a striped petticoat.

A Welsh woman in a nineteenth-century coloured print drawn by an amateur artist has a brown skirt showing a bright red and blue striped petticoat, a white apron, a blue *betgwyn*, a white kerchief patterned in black, a black shawl and a wide-brimmed, flat crowned black hat on which she carries a large basket probably containing butter. She has blue-grey stockings and black shoes which are pushed into wooden pattens with a strap over the ankles. This woman knits stockings as she walks over the high hills. The production of stockings was a village industry, hence the basket balanced on the head, to leave both hands free. She is followed by her son in a green coat of eighteenth-century cut, probably someone's cast-off, high, brown, buttoned gaiters and a black felt hat similar to his mother's. He also has a basket balanced on his head – this contains baby goslings – and he also is knitting stockings.

Loose sleeves were worn with the *betgwyn*. These sleeves, which could be discarded while working, were tied on to the upper-sleeves and were varied in material, colour and design. They can be seen in fifteenth- and sixteenth-century Flemish and Italian illustrations, and in Italy they continued to be worn until rural dress disappeared, and in Holland until the early nineteenth century. In England they were not worn by rural people, which again suggests the link between Welsh dress and the continent. Some of the sleeves in the Cardiff Museum are of printed chintz and are almost identical with the late eighteenth-century examples in the Dutch province of Zeeland.

The Welsh cloak, which succeeded the age-old whittle described earlier, was wider and fuller than the European cloak. It had a very wide hood, resembling those worn by fashionable eighteenth-century ladies. This wide hood could be drawn over the high hat and was sometimes pulled together on top of the hat by ribbon ties.

In an 1814 illustration the red cloak is less ample and more like the

1. *Dress and Manners of the English*, 1814, Victoria and Albert Museum.

English garment, but by the middle of the nineteenth century the more characteristic Welsh garment had developed, often red or deep purple. Another outer covering was the large shawl worn pointed at the back and tied in front.

Lady Llanover's paintings of Welsh costume in the early nineteenth century show fringed shawls, and from these pictures one gathers that the younger women often wore shawls and the older women the big cloaks, but at this period the whittle was also worn; that, too, disappeared in favour of cloaks or shawls.

In all the funeral prints the big cloak was much in evidence, and special ones were hired out for the occasion.

The neck-kerchief was worn in the traditional way, a deep point at the back; and sometimes over and sometimes tucked into the bodice of the *betgwyn*. It was made of various light and patterned materials.

The eighteenth-century head-kerchief was white with a coloured border, pointed at the back and tied under the chin, similar to one shown in an English seventeenth-century print.

Later in the eighteenth and nineteenth centuries linen or muslin coifs were worn, varying in shape but mainly with a single or double frill in front. Mrs. Lois Blake in *Welsh Folk Dance and Costume* describes the coif of the last half of the nineteenth century as being made of a "semi-circle of linen or muslin, can be ironed flat, narrow, with three extra frills all round and three extra frills over the ears. The body of the coif is drawn to the back and fastened with a bow, but is often fastened in front with a bow in a like manner."

Stockings were mostly blue, or striped blue and gray and white. Footless stockings were worn fastened under the heel with a strap; the same type can be seen in a sixteenth-century German print. Many girls walked with bare feet as in the Scottish Highlands and Ireland.

Shoes were strong and black. Clogged pattens were also worn.

Men's dress in the eighteenth and nineteenth centuries, and probably earlier centuries, had no regional characteristics, and as in England followed ordinary fashions in a very minor degree: a cut-away coat, knee-breeches, coarse knitted stockings often tied with a ribbon at the knee.

The cover to Mr. Etheridge's book illustrates an interesting example of the farmer's Sunday suit: red and white waistcoat with a double row of buttons, shirt smocked and frilled at the neck, knee-breeches, the traditional buckled shoes and a brimmed, moderately high-crowned hat. The materials for this costume as well as those of the women would probably be home or locally woven. The Lerry Mills at Talybont[1] has a pattern of material, a grey Welsh wool, probably worn by the men, much the same as that used for the men of Galway, Ireland.

1. Mrs Hughes.

The men wore the traditional brimmed hat of felt, with a square or flat crown. Later a square-crowned and narrow-brimmed hat became fashionable.

Smock-frocks were worn in the nineteenth century, but not so frequently as in England.

Children in some old prints are shown wearing similar dresses to their mothers. Mr. Etheridge in his book has an illustration of a child in a patterned *betgwyn,* flowered and fringed shawl and white frilled coif. This fashion of dressing the children as miniature editions of their parents was prevalent in the Netherlands and Scandinavian countries.

The attractive Welsh dress is now only worn for very special occasions, but every effort is being made to keep it traditionally correct and there are some fine examples of garments in Cardiff and other Welsh museums as well as in private hands.

The National Library of Wales has in its possession patterns of mid-nineteenth-century Welsh flannel, very strong wiry stuff. The basic colours are predominantly black and navy blue, occasionally dark green or orange, and the overlay of plaid, orange and orange-red, royal and light navy blue.

8. Dyes Used by Rural People

The cultivation of plants which could be used for dyeing clothes played a very important part in rural life before the invention of aniline dyes.

Dye plants can be roughly divided into two kinds: the important ones which were extensively cultivated for use in dyeing cloth, linen and silk materials, and those which were gathered by country people for dyeing their own home-woven materials. For the latter purpose plants and lichen mosses would be sought locally. The resultant colours would vary according to the mordant employed and also to the kind of water used in the process of dyeing, whether spring, river or rain water. The time of year when the plant was harvested also had an effect on the colour obtained.

It is impossible to give here all the names of plants that were probably used for dyeing; but the most usual ones will be noted, especially those from which are produced the colours mentioned in chapters on individual garments worn by rural people.

Yellow dye is one of the oldest colours abstracted from plants. It was obtained from the Autumn Crocus – which gave saffron – and weld (*Reseda Luteola*), also known as Dyers Rocket or Wild Mignonette. Saffron was most likely introduced into Europe by the Crusaders. It was always an expensive dye to produce, and therefore was probably not much used by rural workers, unless they lived in a district where saffron grew freely (e.g. Saffron Walden).

According to Worlidge's *Systema Agriculturae* (1669), the English saffron was the best in the world. "Therefore", he continues, "it is to our negligence that it is no more propagated. September flowers appear like a blue crocus (Autumn Crocus)[1]. In the middle of it, two or three chives (stigma) grow upright together, the chives being the very Saffron and no more than you may gather betwixt your fingers and preserve it. It must be done early in the morning, else it returns into the body of the flower again and so for a month's space you may gather two or three crops and then remove it. Care must be taken in drying it in a

1. The saffron is actually made from the stigma of the purple autumnal crocus known as *Crocus Sotivus*.

small kiln of clay and with very little fire and that with careful attendance. Three pounds moist usually making one of dye, sold from 20s. a lb. to £5 a lb. and may cost £4 an acre to manage. An acre bears 7 to 15 lbs."

Joseph Walker, in his *Historical Essay on the Dress of the Ancient and Modern Irish*, quotes Gilbert Anglicus, who says that the saffron plant ash was used in Iceland and Ireland. Walker does not think the plant was indigenous, but imported. Saffron in Ireland was mixed with the bark and leaves of poplar trees beaten together: "They dye their loose shirts to a saffron colour." The bark of an arbutus tree mixed with salt was also used with "Saffron not boiled long, but let soak for some days in urine, that the colour may be deeper and more durable."

The Irish, who were forbidden their saffron-coloured clothes by the English, probably used little of this dye, but substituted lichen. According to Mrs. Mairet, the authority on vegetable dyes, the lichen *Itula Aurata* gives a beautiful saffron yellow, and Violetta Thurstan, in *The Use of Vegetable Dyes* says: "*Pettiyera Canna* with alum as a mordant is a good yellow for linen. Bog Asphodel and Bog Myrtle also give a yellow dye."

Weld, extracted from *Reseda Luteola* or Dyers Rocket, was one of the main dues cultivated on a large scale. Worlidge says: "This is a rich dyer's commodity and grows also in many places in Kent, to very great advantage. It will grow on any ordinary or barren land, so that it will be dry and warm. A gallon of seed will sow an acre on Barley or Oats, very small, and not much the first summer. Cautious in gathering it, seed must not be over-ripe. Pulled, as they do Flax, by the roots, and bound in little handfuls, set to dry and then housed. Beat or lash out the seed, which is of good value, and dispose of the stalk and root to the dyer, which is of singular use for dyeing of bright yellow and lemon colour."

In 1748 the Swedish traveller, Kalm, recorded in his *Account of his visit to England* that *Reseda Luteola* Dyers Weed grew everywhere outside London on the earth walls and that it could be contented with the driest earth. "I noticed from this", he says, "that it grew in fissures in the top of the walls in the greatest heat of the sun, where all other plants were entirely withered up and killed by the great heat, but this stood there green and in flower more than eighteen inches high. The cattle always left it uneaten."

From Gravesend, Kalm writes: "Dyers Weed, which is cultivated for its yellow colour, was in several places drawn up root and all and bound in small sheaves which were set one against another in the fields to dry with Hemp and Flax. It grew here wild in places abundantly, and in other places it was expressly planted."

Dr. Lindemans, the Belgian authority on agriculture[1], says that weld was formerly cultivated in Flanders; "It was grown over the whole country since the Middle Ages, especially round Aalst, Oudenarde and West Brabant, and in the first half of the nineteenth century was still grown in East Flanders. Only with the coming of the aniline dyes did it disappear."

The mordant for weld is alum and cream of tartar, and the time of gathering late summer. Dyer's Greenweed (*Genista Tinctoria*) – another important yellow dye plant – was mixed with woad to give Kendals Green. Fairholt states that the Welsh extracted a beautiful yellow from tansy. Weld yellow was one of the main colours used for working-class clothes. Dr. Lindemans calls it a dull yellow tending towards brown, but I have seen English weld dyeing which was bright yellow.

Woad, the plant, was used in early times to give a blue dye. According to Dr. Lindemans, woad was a two-year crop and the leaves of the blue plant were used. It was cultivated in Limburg and Brabant. It was also used extensively in the fifteenth century. At a very early period it was replaced by indigo, which was imported from India. This was used exclusively for the dyeing of the famous blue cloth of Flanders, and by then woad was only occasionally grown in France and Germany. The latter country, however, used indigo for dyeing their printed blue linen.

Worlidge writes of woad: "The first two crops are the best, usually mixed together in the seasonings. A staple commodity and very advantageous for the dyer's trade. Leaf to be in full growth and lively greenness. Speedily cut it that it fades not nor wax pale before you have cut your crop. Ordinary warm ground."

Other blue dyes are extracted from whortleberry, which is used in the Highlands and gives a purplish blue.

Madder (*Rubra Tinctoria*) was grown mostly in France, Flanders and Holland, but Worlidge says: "Madder was a very rich commodity used in the dyes of red colour, a plant that delights in our climate." He must have meant *Rubra Perigrina*, which grows wild in England and gives a rose dye. *Rubra Tinctoria* does not grow wild, but it may have been cultivated formerly, as red was one of the most important dyes in the Middle Ages and was especially favoured by rural people.

Zeeland, a southern province of the Netherlands, was mentioned in the sixteenth-century Atlas of Ortelius as one of the great producing provinces of madder (*meekrap*). It was used to dye the red baize worn by Breughel's peasants and it continued to be a main crop of Zeeland until the nineteenth century. Madder was grown on the heavy land along the sea coast and was eventually supplanted by the chemical dye alizarin. Madder gives a bright red, brownish red and purplish brown,

1. Lindemans, *Gescheidenis van de Landbouw in Belgie* (1952).

according to the mordant used. Dr. Scrope, in *Extending Planting* (1786) writes; "One row of Madder 8 inch plant to plant. It was set in the experiment ground. Have never viewed plants more luxuriant. Fine crops in two years."

According to Violetta Thurstan, madder is still grown in southern Europe for a beautiful red dye.

Cochineal is produced from the dried bodies of an insect kermes which lives on cactus plants cultivated in Mexico, the Canary Islands and other places. Cochineal gives different shades of crimson, scarlet or rose. This dye, with a mordant of tin and cream of tartar and an admixture of fustic and Persian berries, gives a scarlet wool-dye. Alternatively, tin crystals and oxalic acid crystals can be used to dye wool crimson. Alum and cream of tartar can also be used.[1] Both scarlet and crimson wool were largely used by rural people in western Europe for their clothing.

Cochineal was first imported from America in the sixteenth century, and from about 1630 to 1830 in any list of rural clothing you will find red as one of the main colours. Madder was also used, especially wherever the plant was plentiful, but the French word *ecarlate,* the Netherlands *scharlaken,* the German *scharlach,* and the English stammel designated both the colour scarlet and scarlet cloth. The German word *scharlach* is also used for cochineal.

In the eighteenth and nineteenth centuries both madder and cochineal were used for the heavy skirts and petticoats of the rural women. It was used too in Switzerland and Norway for the partlet which covered the breast. Cochineal may have been used to dye the bright red of the eighteenth- and early nineteenth-century English and Welsh cloaks – the Cardinal cloak of the lowland Scots. Cochineal will also give purple red and violet, according to the mordant used.

Manx women dyed their petticoats dark red with lichen. This plant produced greys and browns – the colours most often mentioned in connection with earlier dresses. Norway, Sweden, Iceland, the Shetlands, Orkney and Skye, and the Western Islands used lichens for dyeing. Such plants were used until quite lately for dyeing Harris, Shetland and Donegal tweeds. Violetta Thurstan gives a list of ten different lichens used for dyeing. *Lecanoca Tartarea,* she says, was used as a red dye by the peasants of Wales, the Shetlands and the Orkneys.

Orchil and Cudbear, also lichens, give beautiful shades of red and purple; Orchil was an old continental dye.

Blackberry gives bluish grey for wool.

Onion skins give a golden brown.

Fairholt says that the Welsh used the leaves of foxgloves.

Logwood was much used for dyeing browns and blacks.

1. Violetta Thurstan, *The Use of Vegetable Dyes.*

Glossary

Bay: Reddish Brown.

Boys or Boyes: A napped woollen material, medieval, lighter than modern baize.

Broadcloth: A fine woollen cloth of plain weave. This is probably the hard-wearing cloth called Manchester (Cunnington). It was worn by the peasant men of Zeeland (Netherlands) in the nineteenth and twentieth centuries.

Buckram: A cloth stiffened with gum.

Buriat: A thick rough woollen cloth.

Buskins: High boots worn by countrymen.

Calimanco: Material of wool and silk.

Camlet: A stuff of wool or goat's hair (Cunnington).

Canvas: A textile of hemp or coarse linen, much used for working aprons.

Capa: A hooded cloak.

Chin Clout: A piece of white material covering the mouths of English and German countrywomen in the fifteenth and sixteenth centuries when going to market, especially in the early morning, and probably as a protection against wind and damp.

Choppinos: High wooden pattens covered in leather. In some cases painted. Origin in China.

Clouts: Napkins. Kerchief "with homely clouts and knitted on their heads". Also patches as applied to boots or shoes; in some cases the reference is to the clouts or nails on shoes.

Cockers: High laced boots worn by countrymen, mentioned by Piers Plowman. Later in the north of England the word was used for gaiters or leggings or even for coarse stockings without feet.

Cogware: A coarse narrow cloth like frieze.

Coif: Close head-dress, worn in medieval times by men and women, but later by most countrywomen of western Europe and the British Isles.

Cote: A kind of tunic or frock. Chaucer writes: "The yeoman was clad in a cote." "The miller in a white cote."

Coverchif: A veil for covering the head.

Dowlas: Coarse and sometimes fine linen material for shirts and aprons. *Chichester Archives;* (John Bridges, Tailor, 1721): "Order 2 pieces of fine Dowlas".

Duffel: A coarse woollen stuff, blue or scarlet baize: seventeenth century (Cunnington).

Durrance or Duretta: A strong kind of stuff worn in the sixteenth and seventeenth centuries. Durrance petticoats for women.

Fallingbands: A kind of falling ruff or plain band worn in the seventeenth century.

Faylding or Faldying: A coarse cloth like frieze for rough external purpose. Coarse redcloth was still woven and dyed for petticoats and jackets by Irishwomen in the nineteenth century.

Felt hats were worn in England by the ordinary people from the Middle Ages until the nineteenth century. Beaver hats worn by the wealthier countrymen, and were introduced at the time of Elizabeth I. They were made from a mixture of fibres of fur and wool.

Ferret: A narrow worsted ribbon for binding dresses in the seventeenth to nineteenth centuries.

Fore- or Foot-mantle: A petticoat used by market-women when they rode horseback to keep their gowns clean.

Frieze: A coarse woollen cloth thick and narrow for jerkins, doublets and gowns particularly in the sixteenth century. Fuller in his *Worthies* (1662) writes that it was made in Wales.

Frock: Tunic of countrymen.

Fur: Peasants wore cat, badger and red squirrel.

Fustian: Cotton cloth used by the Normans. It was very strong and was used for jackets and doublets in the fifteenth century. Wool fustian was made in Norwich, 1330.
Another definition: A fabric of cotton and flax or flax mixed with wool and having a silky finish, very popular with all classes. In *Chichester Archives,* 1721 (John Bridges, Tailor) is recorded an order for 80 yards coloured fustian, 1 piece and half of white fustian.

Gaiters: Seventeenth century; leather fitting closely and worn with shoes.

Galoche: Wooden shoes or pattens made all in one piece and fastened to the foot with thongs of leather and worn by poorer classes in winter. Chaucer: "No were worthy remake his galoche".

Gamashes: Sixteenth century; high boots, buskins or start-ups.

Hanselen: A sort of loose jacket or "slop" mentioned in Chaucer.

Hemp seed: Grown a great deal in England and Flanders, for a coarse linen cloth. The districts where it was grown in England was Suffolk and the district of Holland in Lincolnshire.

Holland Cloth: A linen cloth.

Hooks and Eyes, and *Crochettes and Loops:* Known in the fourteenth century.

Huik Haiek, etc: An outer garment or mantle worn by women from the fourteenth to the seventeenth century in parts of Europe and occasionally in England, (for other variations see page 109).

Inkle: A narrow woollen tape used for trimming a dress or hat, usually yellow but sometimes striped blue and pink or blue and red – "An old country woman with inkle about her hat" (1677).

Jacket, Jaquet, Jerkin or *Coat:* Names for same garment.

Kendals Green: Coarse green woollen stuff.

Kersey: A coarse narrow woollen cloth.

Kerseymere: A cloth from Kersey, Suffolk; also made in Devonshire.

Kirtle: A loose gown, tunic or waistcoat.

Linsey-Woolsey: Coarse woollen cloth.

Lockram: Coarse linen cloth loosely woven, with relatively finer varieties used for skirt, neck wear, coifs of the poorer class (Cunnington).

Mockado: Much used in sixteenth and seventeenth centuries and made from hemp seed.

Partlett: A gorget for women, a neckerchief, a rail and many other things. In countrywomen's dress it covered the breast above the bodice and was worn under various names in most west European countries.

Patten: A shaped wooden sole, fitted after the seventeenth century with iron rings on under-side. Used by countrywomen in England to protect their shoes.

Petticoats: Undergarments, but word was also used in sixteenth and early seventeenth centuries for top skirt. Red stammel was often used for petticoats.

Pinner: Apron with bib pinned in front of dress, pin cloth or pinafore.

Placard: Stomacher, a piece of material worn in front, curved at waist, in the first half of the fifteenth century, but retained in rural costume under the laced corset-bodice, particularly in Switzerland and Norway, and given a variety of names.

Pouch: Bag or receptacle worn by countrywomen hanging from the girdle.

Puce: Purple brown.

Rugg(e): A coarse woollen stuff for poorer people.

Russett: Reddish brown or grey. A coarse homespun cloth called friar's cloth or shepherd's clothing made from hemp. Both colour and cloth were much worn by country people.

Saffron: Extracted from stigma of the autumn crocus, was grown in Saffron Walden, but was mostly imported. It was expensive and probably not much used for rural clothing.

Satines: A cheap kind of satin (Cunnington).

Seak cloth: Sack cloth.

Serge: A coarse woollen cloth. (cf. Fairholt – a twilled cloth of worsted or worsted and wool, seventeenth century.) "*Serdge,*" black was worn by English seamen and was mentioned in 1602 in a letter to Sir Walter Raleigh from John Breton.

Slops: A loose outer garment, jacket, tunic, smock-frock. Chaucer speaks of kitted sloppes and Caxton of a new sloppe. In the nineteenth century a smock-frock was called a "Waggoner's slop". The word was also used for the wide Dutch breeches which originated in the sixteenth century and were worn by seamen, and fishermen especially in the Netherlands, during the sixteenth century. The word was used for baggy breeches and hose, everything loose fitting; hence the English word "sloppy"

Smock: A women's undergarment, a shift or chemise. Cambric smocks were mentioned in *Marstone Malcontent,* 1604. Smock as a term for the smock-frock was only used after 1800.

Stammel: A word used for a red cloth, sometimes for the colour of the cloth. This double meaning where red cloth is concerned is found in French *écarlate,* meaning both red and cloth, and *scharlaken* in Dutch, for cloth and colour was much used by rural people for various garments in their regional dresses from the seventeenth to the nineteenth centuries.

Start-up: High shoes or gamashes for country folk.

Sticken Pins: Knitting needles for nether stocking.

Stocking "Hole": In many illustrations of early peasant hose or stockings made of woven material a deliberate hole was cut out over the knee cap. At first I thought this might be intended as an indication of poverty, until I found that this custom was prevalent in many countries prior to the introduction of knitted stockings. It is quite understandable, since knitted stockings "give" and when a hole does appear it can be darned, whereas material merely rubs and can only be patched, and a hand-sewn patch over the knee cap is likely to wear very quickly.

The earliest illustration I have found of this "hole" is a Byzantine boy bowling a hoop. His hose, worn with laced sandals, has a definite round hole cut out over his knee cap.

The Winchester Bible (1140-60) has two unusual examples; they are both at the back of the leg on the calf and are oval in shape.

In the Italian fourteenth-century *Tacuinum Sanitatis* herbal workers nearly all have hose with knee-holes, mostly rather jagged, and the edges to these footless stockings are also jagged. One man's hose-holes are neater and his more solid hose are thrust into high shoes. As he wears a hooded cape, this was probably a winter costume. Three German countrymen of the late fifteenth century have diamond-shaped holes over their knees.

The "Prodigal Son" in the Hieronymus Bosch picture (late fifteenth century) also has a hole in his grey hose, and in a Leiden Psalter of 1440 the holes are round.

The Scottish sixteenth-century shepherd has short hose with knee-holes with jagged edges.

The last example I have found is dated 1638 and is of a German shepherd in a picture by Brenck the Younger. His clothing is that of a poor man and the hose are footless and jagged and the knee hole is big.

A Swiss print of 1744, however, shows contemporary central European soldiers with such three-holes.

Tabard: A loose upper garment of coarse material, a variety of tunic, hanging from the shoulders, slit up the sides, with and without sleeves. The seams were sometimes sewn together. The opening was wide. Date fourteenth to sixteenth century.

The ploughman in Chaucer's *Canterbury Tales* rode on his mare in a tabard. "The Shepherd upon a hill he sat, he had on him his tabard and his hat." *(Piers Plowman)* The water carrier in the early sixteenth century wore a tabard.

Water Carrier: Though this is not strictly a rural costume, it is an outdoor costume that has been seldom described and seems to be indigenous to England.

Wimple: A covering for the neck, forming part of the coif.

Woad: In early days, a blue dye for wool, preceding indigo.

Worsted: A woollen cloth, often used for hose or stockings.

Appendix I

Sumptuary Laws of Switzerland, Germany, Flanders, The Netherlands, France, Italy, England, Ireland and Norway

Sumptuary laws are of the greatest importance when describing early rural dress. The main difficulty is to find sufficient published information. The chief sources from which information can be obtained are as follows:

Swiss laws and some from southern Germany are fully transcribed and recorded in *Costume and Custom in Basle, Berne and Zürich*, by John Martin Vincent.

Sumptuary Laws of Legislation of England, by Baldwin, *The Dress of the Ancient and Modern Irish*, by Joseph C. Walker (1787), and *Old Irish and Highland Dress* by McClintock, give details of rural dress in the British Isles and the effects of sumptuary laws.

An article on *Peasant Art in Italy*, by S. J. C. Churchill, published in *The Studio* in 1913, gives some information on Italian laws.

Roger-Miles' *Costume de France* gives a note on the laws of Henry II.

There are a few other odd references to the subject in print.

M. le Juge Mahillon has transcribed for me the Flemish laws of Charles V (1550). The Flanders laws of 1550 probably applied to Holland as well, but after the Reformation no trace can be found of any sumptuary laws in the northern Netherlands: the peasants there were considerably freer from restrictive laws than in most western European countries, and such restriction as was applied to keep rural costume free from extravagance and indecency was directed by the Calvinist church. There are probably many interesting laws hidden away in local archives well worth transcribing on the lines of that most informative book by John Martin Vincent[1]. It is from this work that one realises the tremendous influence Swiss sumptuary laws had on rural costume. The main reason for applying these laws was to stop the peasants from wearing imported goods and to force them to use native materials, thus avoiding expenditure of scarce money on unnecessary luxuries.

---

1. *Costume and Custom in Basle, Berne and Zürich* (1935).

Switzerland

Sumptuary laws also give an idea of the sort of clothes that were worn, the names for garments and materials, and their dates. In Switzerland the laws were regional, varied from place to place, and were administered by the councillors with a certain amount of paternal feeling. They affected all classes except the nobles. Fines were imposed for non-compliance, and there was a good deal of evasion. The fines were probably often paid by the middle class for the privilege of wearing a bit of finery, but peasants were not as a rule in a position to part with the little money they possessed. This is probably the reason why the dress remained so conservative until the last quarter of the eighteenth century, when it became freer and at the same time more regional.

With the coming of the French Revolution the sumptuary laws concerning clothing were abolished, and this had an immediate effect on the dress of both men and women in the greater part of western Europe. Rural clothes became gayer and more elaborate and remained so until they disappeared at the end of the nineteenth century.

The following are some points from the sumptuary laws which apply to rural communities: (The earliest law quoted by Vincent is Zürich 1370.)

1370 – The dress to be so close-fitting in the neck that the opening should only be two inches on the shoulder, no buttons or lacings permitted.

1482 – Under income of 1000 gilders, no belt with metal mountings, no silk borders to bodice, no hooks or buckles.

1488 – The outer garments of men and boys to reach to the knee. For women, silk borders on bodices allowed, but no hooks or buckles.

To the end of the fifteenth century short garments were not allowed, nor was gold nor silver slashing. Expensive jewellery was forbidden.

In the fourteenth century leg hose must not be striped or made of cloth of different colours.

1628 – Peasants were to avoid "a multitude of cords" lying close together on their clothing, including waistcoats and breeches. Sleeves were to be made of cloth or woollen material suitable to the class of the wearer. Servants were forbidden to wear great, long or thick ruffs. Women were forbidden to wear their hair dressed high and their sleeves slashed. Men must not have thick curled hair.

They were allowed to wear leather, corduroy, Wendish or Basle cloth and double buriat. Mock velvet was forbidden. Servants might only have one stripe on their dress and generally might carry no gold or silver knives. No coral or things that had the appearance of gold or silver might be worn round the neck. Ruffs were to be limited in size and, in place of fur trimming, only black wool from sheepskins could be used.

Cost of hoods was limited to two gulden and this must include lining, "fur" and cost of making. Hats must be of simple felt, plain and no cords on them: they must be small and ribbon rosettes must not cost more than one shilling.

Peasants were forbidden to go out with girdle belts which had ornaments and knife sheath attached.

Stockings must be of cheap cloth or *Pariser Strumph*. Shoes to be made of common leather, without heels and not to be perforated.

Maidens must have felt hats with only a little thread work, and only simple ribbons or borders might be worn; but for their weddings they were allowed wreaths on their hats, with "lawful" dress or jackets.

1637 – No Netherlands linen; only homespun for ruffs. No solid silver for wives and children. Only plain gold wedding ring. One stripe only, and two quiltings on sleeves and jackets. Dresses should have not more than three stripes (an advancement on the one stripe of 1628!) Hats to be of inferior marten skin.

Tuchli (the native coif) to be worn all day by maidservants. On Sundays cloak and *Tuchli* could be worn. (This was probably the general rural dress, as maids usually came from peasant families, as they do today in many western European countries.)

In the last half of the seventeenth century children might not have any garment of silk, satin, plush or new scarlet cloth. Girls' bonnets might not be more than three inches wide but could be decorated. High Bernoise coifs were not allowed.

1708 – Plain ribbon on edge of skirt allowed; also shoes of leather, felt or cloth.

Servants to keep their costume as long as possible. Neither man- nor maidservant might wear a silk neckcloth or scarf, but only a simple ironed collar.

1708 – Only coifs and hoods of simple native cloth to be worn. Peasant lace was permitted. Shoes must be black or oiled. Velvet, silk, brocade or linen velvet in any colour or form forbidden, with the exception of facings on basques or sleeves. Prayer-books decorated with gold were also forbidden.

1715 – Short garments were forbidden.

1744 to 1797 – Street dresses might be made of wool, cotton or linen. Head-dresses and neck scarves of plain black gauze and taffeta without lace or fringe might be worn. Dresses of black buriat with apron of the same material were also allowed, but the "lower orders" might not wear satin or damask.

On women's coifs silver or gold Swiss lace might not be more than an inch wide. There must be no exposure of shoulders, and collars were to be closed. At 15 girls must wear women's dress.

A big advance in 1780, when it was decreed that dresses might be of silk, though not of muslin or velvet.

By 1797 the restrictions were still severe, but prosecutions were rare. With the advent of the French Revolution all costume laws came to an end.

Germany

Mr. Martin Vincent thinks that many of the Swiss laws would apply to south Germany.

I have found in Hottenroth's *Deutsche Volkstracht*, Vols I and II, the following laws:

1200 – Gloves, swords and spears were forbidden.

In the early fifteenth century the wearing of red, blue or green was forbidden; therefore neutral colours – black, grey or brown – were worn.

In spite of these laws, the peasants at the end of the fifteenth century wore a good deal of finery. Consequently, gold, pearls, silk and damask were forbidden; also certain cloths of special colours. The price that might be paid for cloth was limited.

A Berlin Order of 1486 decreed that the "lower orders" (which always included peasants) had to cover their heads with their cloaks; otherwise they were daring to imitate the Emperor's cloak. In the Rhineland ordinary men might not wear mantles; women might not wear short clothing, nor, in summer, short aprons, chemises, foreign or conspicuous clothing.

Flanders

1545 – January 30th. Vassals or "lower orders" might not wear tabard or velvet, satin or damask of any colour, nor cramoisy, nor gold or silver cloth. Brocade, silver embroidery, border of *passementerie*, fringes of gold and silver, velvet, satin or taffeta trimmed or embroidered with gold or silver were all forbidden. Peasants might not wear *wambuessen* (jerkins) of silk or *casquins* (loose coats) embroidered or puffed with silk, or any kind of silk.

1550 – Ordnance of Charles v. May 27th.

The Netherlands

The following information was given me by Mr. de Bree of Middleburg,

Walcheren, Zeeland. It concerns a sumptuary law enacted in the northern Netherlands when that country was under the rule of the French King Louis Napoleon.

June 6th, 1809 – From the first of the Haymonth (July) is forbidden the wearing of more than one *oorijzer plaat* (the ornament attached to the head band supporting the coif) by any woman of the province of Zeeland. Married women to wear the ornament on the left side, unmarried women on the right. Only women who suckled their children themselves were allowed to wear two. (The ordinance uses the word *oorijzer*, but the flat gold ornament, the *plaat* was probably meant. This *plaat* was worn by the peasants of Zeeland from the end of the eighteenth to well into the nineteenth century.)

The mother who has suckled most children shall be presented by the oldest member of the rural council with a head band with two golden *plaaten* on June 1st. The villagers, especially the young women, shall be invited to this ceremony. A sports competition for young men should follow the ceremony; the cost of the prizes to be borne by the Minister of the Interior.

France

I have found only two French ordinances. One is in a verse by Ronsard, cited by Roger-Miles in his *Costume de France* congratulating Roi Henri on making a barrier between classes by forbidding the use of velvet and silk to certain classes of people:

> *"Le Velour trop common en France Sous Toy reprend son viell honneur"*

The other is a thirteenth-century ordinance: lower orders may not wear buttons made of gold and silver or other metals; by Royal decree only cloth, thread covered buttons.

Italy

PROVINCE OF AREZZO: *1568* – A peasant woman was not allowed to wear silk garments, except a silk net for the hair, a silk bonnet (coif), silk ribbons and girdles of silk. Her necklace might not exceed three scudi in value, nor might her girdle cost more than three scudi; but she could wear two gold rings of the same value. A rosary costing one scudo was permitted. She could have velvet, silk or damask for the trimming of bodice, petticoat and sleeves, and any other non-prohibited stuff might be used. Hats of silk or straw were allowed. No gold ornaments except rings were permitted.

TUSCANY: Silk garments, necklace of silver beads, girdle of velvet, silver studs, silver gilt buckles, silver buckles and silver gilt bodkins: all these things were permitted.

PISA: Material for the outer garments was limited to cloth, with a pair of cloth sleeves. The following could be worn in addition: a girdle of velvet with silver gilt mount and its bodkin, silver gilt rings, a pendant cross of silver gilt hanging from a silken band, straw hat, chemise, collar, cuffs, cap or coif, and an apron. All could be ornamented with linen but not with silk.

PISTLIA: *1558* – Regulations were strict, but a wreath was allowed in the hair.

Sumptuary laws in Italy regulated peasant attire at weddings as well as at baptisms.

These details give some idea of the richness of the Italian rural dress, which has always been the most elaborate and has the most continuous tradition in western Europe.

England (cf. Baldwin's *Sumptuary Laws of Legislation of England*). The first sumptuary law with reference to clothing was in *1363* regulating the dress of various classes.

1404 – People with very small incomes – less than 40s. a year – shall not wear any fustian or bustian.

1483 – No yeoman of the Manor or anyone else below the rank of squire or gentleman was allowed to wear on his doublet damask, satin or camlet.

Servants in husbandry (agricultural labourers), common labourers, servants and handicraft men living outside the cities or boroughs, and their wives, were prohibited from wearing common cloth if it cost more than 2s. 3d. Wives of servants in husbandry were forbidden to wear kerchiefs costing more than 20d. the plight.

Men were not to wear hose costing more than 18d. the pair, and were fined 40d. for disobeying this ordinance.

1464 – People with small incomes (of not more than 40s. a year) might not wear fustian, bustian or scarlet cloth, and only black and white lamb skin, and no other fur was allowed.

1509 – No one who could not claim title of gentleman was allowed to wear furs imported from abroad, or chain or ornament of fine gold. No servants, yeomen and persons with an income of less than 40s. a year might wear hose made of cloth worth more than 2s. a yard. Coifs and bonnets worn by servants and yeomen must not be embroidered or trimmed with silk, gold or silver.

Strutt quotes fifteenth-century sumptuary laws:

No yeoman, or under degree of yeoman, shall wear apparel of his body any bolster nor stuffing of wool, cotton or caddis in his pourpoint or doublet but a lining according to same. No wives shall wear a square, or girdles garnished with silver.

Woollen bonnets are excepted in clause forbidding woollen cloth from abroad.

Ireland

The sumptuary laws of the preceding countries were made for three reasons: to prevent extravagance amongst the rural population, to encourage home-spun textiles from home-grown seed and to emphasise the rights of the nobility.

The Irish laws had a fourth and very important purpose: to overcome Irish reluctance to become part of England, by suppressing what was a very distinctive Irish way of dressing. By these laws the Irish were made to adopt the English style of clothing.

The Irish dress – primitive but exceedingly traditional – was based on the early Gaelic-Frankish and certainly Norse costumes. The Irish did retain, after the introduction of the sumptuary laws, certain indigenous rural elements in their dress. But the main influence thereafter was mainly western European until all rural costume disappeared from use.

From Joseph Walker's *Historical Essay on the Dress of the Ancient and Modern Irish* (1787):

1565 – No inhabitant dwelling within the Mitre and being a free man or woman to wear no apparel but after the English fashion, nor no woman to wear caps again upon forfeiture, that every burgess and every freeman shall go in his cloak – (short cloak in the English fashion).

Prohibition of the wearing of the Mantle and Trouse to all people.

WEST MEATH: Disappearance of Irish Cap, mantle and trouse in certain counties. Prohibition of garments made of a sort of narrow frieze. Dress that the Irish might wear: *bendel* (band), neckerchief, mocket or linen cap.

The Deputy Governor of Galway issued an order to prohibit wearing of the mantle to all people whatsoever, "which law was executed with great vigour, and from that time mantle and trouse were disused for the most part."

GALWAY. Letter of Henry VII: "No man or man child to wear mantles in the streets, but cloak or gowns or doublet or hose after the English fashion. No man or woman or child to wear in their shirt or smock or any other garment saffron. (This colour, saffron yellow, was the main feature of the Irish costume.) Nor to have any more cloth in their garment, but five ells standard of that country – handymen and labourers ten cubits of linen cloth permitted."

MUNSTER: *1571* – Inhabitants of cities or corporate towns shall wear no mantles, Irish coats or great shirts, nor suffer their hair to grow, but to wear clerks gowns, jackets or jerkins. No maid or single woman shall wear or put any roll or kerchief of linen upon her head, neither any great smock with sleeves, but put on hats, French hoods, tippets or some other civil attire upon her head. Hair not to be worn in Irish fashion or long. Short smock, *bendel* (band or ribbon), neckchief, *toocket* (bib or handkerchief), linen cap, coloured or dyed with saffron. No more than seven yards of cloth to be used.

May 1st, 1539: No woman to wear "kyrtell" or *cote* tuckered or embroidered with silk or "couched" (overlaid or embroidered) with "usker" (*usgar*, a jewel or ornament after Irish fashion). No person to wear mantles, *cote* or hood after Irish fashion, but mantles, *cote* after English fashion.

Norway

In *The Norseman*, J. P. Harthan writes of Norwegian folk costume in the Romantic age: "An unending series of sumptuary laws, most ineffective, were framed to prevent the peasants and lower classes from wearing finery which distinguished their "betters". If a peasant were to dress like a gentleman he might be thought to be one, with a consequent blurring of the social structure."

The sumptuary laws for rural clothing were severe between the end of the fourteenth century and the end of the sixteenth century, a period which coincides with the peasants' release from serfdom and gradual, though not complete freedom and the possibility of acquiring their own farms and therefore becoming more of a power in the land.

Particularly at the end of the sixteenth century, there are many complaints in various western European countries, that the rural people were aping the townspeople and even the nobility in their love of finery. This was probably not only a class feeling, but a fear that the precarious economy of those days would be upset, and this was most likely the cause of the spate of clothing laws.

By the seventeenth century most European countries were so devastated by wars that the land and the farms were affected, and the fashions of the rural dresses remained more or less static until the last quarter of the eighteenth century, when the dress developed regionally and freely according to personal income.

Appendix II

The Costume of the Bedewomen of the Trinity Hospital at Castle Rising

This hospital was founded by Henry Howard, Earl of Northampton, in 1616 to house twelve poor and old women from three local villages. Their costume, worn over a very long period, dates from the foundation. The earliest dress seems to have been made of blue fustian lined with baize, and with this gown was worn a high crowned hat, probably black and most likely with a white coif under it. Linsey gowns are mentioned in the hospital's account books of 1648 and again in 1749. Brown gowns are often mentioned and 1s. 6d. was paid for one in 1749.

The colour is interesting, as it is often mentioned in costume records as being a poor person's colour, and brown was worn a great deal by countrywomen in western Europe.

In the seventeenth century the baize lining for gowns cost 2s. to 2s. 4d. a yard. In 1634, 84 yards of black frieze was bought. Black gowns are very rarely mentioned, so we can presume that these gowns were worn for mourning, probably in connection with the founder family of Northampton.

In 1620, sand-coloured marble cloth at 13s. a yard was bought for the Governess's (Matron's) dress; it was also lined with baize.

In 1863 there is the first mention of the scarlet cloth, which was used to make the newly adopted cloaks. The cost was £8 13s. 6d., and £7 6s. was paid for the making. These cloaks are still worn for Church on Sunday and are definitely of the same shape and colour as the eighteenth- and nineteenth-century English, lowland Scottish (the Cardinal cloak) and some types of Welsh cloak. The Castle Rising cloak is made of scarlet serge (?) with a deep hood edged with braid of the same colour, identical with those depicted in eighteenth- and nineteenth-century paintings. The only difference is that the Hospital cloak has the crest of the Northampton family embroidered on the front.

My guess is that the late adoption of the cloak was due to a revolt by the sisters against the wearing of the old-fashioned heavy cloth baize-lined gown. They probably asked for a more modern and lighter type of dress. These dresses would need an outdoor garment, and what more natural than to adopt the rural scarlet cloak still in use, and England's one national garment?

In 1961, the sisters refused to wear the very heavy and conspicuous hats for Sunday church, and these have now been replaced by a more up-to-date model. The original high hat of 1616 most likely resembled that worn by Lucas de Heere's 1574 *English Country Woman* or the one in the *Album Amicorum* miniature of an English peasant (1623).

The late Miss Francis Pitt, the well known ornithologist, owned an old print of Jane Scrimshaw which is inscribed with the following words: "Jane Scrimshaw, daughter of Thomas Scrimshaw, wool stapler of Bow, A.D. 1581, April ye 3rd, is alive and very healthy this present year 1710 att ye Merchant Taylors Alm House on Little Tower Hill." This remarkable old lady wears a hat identical to those worn by the Sisters of the Trinity Hospital, Castle Rising. The Merchant Taylor's Alm House has now been financed for some time by the Mercers Company of London: unfortunately the records of the Merchant Taylors do not mention any particular costume.

NOTE

There are now two authentic Scarlet Cloaks on view:
1. Worcestershire County Museum, Hartlebury Castle, Worcester.
2. The Gallery of English Costume, Platt Hall, Rusholme, Manchester.

Bibliography

GENERAL

Bodleian Library, Oxford; Douce Collection of Prints, 1830
Bossert, H.; *Peasant Art in Europe and Asia,* 1959
Bradley, Caroline; *History of World Costume,* 1955
Braun, Georgius & Hogenberg, Franz; *Civitates Orbis Terrarum, 1572-1618,* 1612 ed.
British Museum; *Album Amicorum,* 17th C.
Brooklyn Botanic Gardens; *Dye Plants and Dyeing* – a handbook, 1964
Bruhn, Wolfgang & Tilke, Max; *A Pictorial History of Costume,* 1955
Bruyn, A. de; *Habitus Variarum Gentium, 1581,* 1885 ed.

Davenport, M.; *The Book of Costume,* 1948
Douce Collection; see under Bodleian Library

Harleian Collection, British Museum; History of Shoe-making
Hartley, Dorothy; *Mediaeval Life and Costume,* 1931
Hollar, Wenceslaus; *Voyages, c.* 1640

Kelly, F. M. & Schwabe, R.; *Historic Costume,* 1925

Lacroix, Paul; *Moeurs et Usages du Moyen Age,* 1871
Leloir, M.; *Histoire du Costume,* 1933-49

Planché, J. R.; *A Cyclopaedia of Costume,* 1876
Planché, J. R.; *Library of Entertaining Knowledge,* 1884

(Symposium); *People of all Nations, c.* 1922

Thurstan, Violetta; *The Use of Vegetable Dyes,* 1949

Vico, Enea; *Recueil de la Diversité des Habits qui sont de présent en usage dans les pays de l'Europe,* 1562
Victoria and Albert Museum; *Galerie royale de costumes* (lithographs), 1827
von Boehn, Max; *Modes and Manners,* 1932

Weiditz, C.; *Das Trachtenbuch des Christoph Weiditz von seinen Reisen nach Spanien, 1529, und der Niederländen 1531-2,* 1927
Wright, T.; *Romance of the Shoe c.* 1860

AUSTRIA

Lepage, E. Medvey; *Costume of Austria and Hungary,* 1939

Reichner, Herbert; *Original Tyrolean Costume,* 1937

BALTIC STATES

Heikel, Aexel O.; *Volkstracht in den Ostenprovinzen,* 1900

BELGIUM

Bibliothèque Nationale, Bruxelles; *Heures de Notre Dame de Hennessey,* 16th C.

Cabinets d'Estampes et Beaux Arts; *Hendricus Rubens,* J. Siebrechts 17th C.

Friedländer, Max J.; *Early Netherlands Painting: Van Eyck to Breughel,* 1956

Hoyois, Giovanni; *Ardennes et Les Ardennais,* 1953

Lindemans, Dr. Paul; *Gescheidenis van de Landbouw in Belgie,* 1952

Madou, J.; *Costume de Belgique, c.* 1830

Sterkers-Ceiters, Dr. Paula; *Volksdracht in Vlaanderen,* (Ghent University Library), 20th C.

BYZANTIUM

Osward, Maxim; *Asia Minor,* 1958

Stark, Freya; *Alexander's Path,* 1958

DENMARK

Andersen, Ellen; *Folk Costume of Denmark,* 1952

Braun, Georgius and Hogenberg, Franz; *Civitates Orbis Terrarum, 1572-1618,* 1612 ed.

Fabricus, R. L.; *Danemark – Holland,* 1948

Hinte, Dr. J. van; *Een Nederlandse Nederzetting in Danemark,* 1938

Mygdal, Elna; *Amagerdragter,* 1930

Nydel, Tage Hansen; *Amager: The Story of an Island,* 1946

FRANCE

Bazin; *Le Livre des Saisons* (Skira ed.) 1918
Blum, André; *The Last Valois*, 1951
(Bodleian Library, Oxford); *Roman de la Rose*, 14th C.

Darjou, A., & Leroux, M.; *Costume de la Bretagne*, 1865
Descerpcz, François; *Receuil de la Diversité des Habits* (Paris), 1567

Gardilanne, G. de and Moffat, Helen; *Les Costumes Régionaux de la France* 1929

Grasset de Saint Sauveur; *Costume de Provence Français*, 18th C.
(Most Museum Libraries); *Les Très Riches Heures du Duc de Berry* (reprinted), late 14th C.
Le Brévaire de Philippe le Bon, 16th C.

Racinet; *Costume Historique*, 1880
Roger-Miles, L.; *Costume de France: Comment descerner les Styles du* VIII au XIX *siècle*, 19th C.

Stothard, Mrs. Charles; *Letters written during a Tour of Normandy and Brittany*, 1820

GERMANY

Amman, Jobst; Book of engravings of European costume 1570-80 (Brighton Reference Library)

Baur-Heinhold, Margarete & Retzlaff, Erich; *Deutsche Trachten*, 1958

Diedrichs; *Deutsches Leben in Bilderein*, 1908

Hamann, Richard; *Geschichte der Kunst*, 1952
Helm, Rudolph; *Germanischen Museum in Nürnberg*, 1936
Helm, Rudolph; *Hessische Bauerntrachten*, 1932
Hottenroth, F.; *Deutsche Volkstracht* (French ed., 1888-1892), 1912 ed.

Julien, R.; *Deutsche Volkstracht*, 1912

Lipperheide; *Historische Volkstracht*, 1890

Mautner, Konrad; *Steirische Trachtenbuch* (2 vols.), 1932

Pettigrew, D. W.; *Peasant Costume of the Black Forest*, 1937

Tilke, M.; *Costumes of Eastern Europe*, 1926

GREAT BRITAIN

Ackermann; *Third Tour of Dr. Syntax*, 1822

Ackermann; *World in Miniature,* 1825

Album Amicorum (Egerton Ms. British Museum), early 17th C.

Anonymous; *Picturesque Representations of the Dress and Manners of the English,* 1814

Anonymous; *Twelve plates of Welsh Peasantry,* 1850

Ashton, John; *Ballad, Humour, Wit and Satire,* 1883

Bagford Ballads; Collected by J. W. Ebsworth (British Museum), 1876-78

Baldwin, F. E.; *Sumptuary Laws of Legislation of England,* 1926

Becket, J. R.; *Sussex County Magazine:* article on smock-frocks

Bell, Vicars; *To Meet Mr. Ellis,* 1956

Blake, Lois; *Welsh Folk Dance and Costume,* 1954

British Museum; *Album Amicorum,* early 17th C.
  Bagford Ballads, collected by J. W. Ebsworth, 1876-78
  Bedford Book of Hours, 1423
  Egerton Ms. (*Album Amicorum*), early 17th C.
  Harleian Collection: *Shepherds' Calendar,* 1774
  Heere, Lucas de: Irish and English Costume, 1574
  Luttrell Psalter, 14th C.
  Roxburghe Collection of Ballads, 1560-1700
  Worlidge, John: *Systema Agriculturae,* 1669-1675

Brome, J.; *Travels in England, Scotland and Wales,* 1700

Brown, Ivor; *Balmoral,* 1955

Butler, Samuel; *Hudibras,* 1663

Cambrensis, Giraldus; *Topography of Ireland and Wales* (translated by R. C. Hoare)

Cunnington, C. W.; *Handbook of English Medieval Costume,* 1952

Cunnington, C. W.; *Handbook of English Costume in the 16th Century* 1954

Ellis, Megan; "Dress and Dress Materials for a Serving Maid, circa 1600." *Journal of National Library of Wales,* Vol. I No. 2. Winter 1939

Etheridge, Ken; *Welsh Costume,* 1958

Fairholt, F. W.; *English Costume,* 1846, 1896

Fitzherbert, A.; *Book of Husbandrie,* 1523

Gombe, W.; *Tour of Dr. Syntax,* 1812

Grimm, S. H.; *Topography of England,* 1770-90

Grant, I. F.; *Everyday Life in Scotland,* 1931-32

Hailstone, Edward; *Costume of Yorkshire,* 1885

Harrison, David; *Tudor England,* 1953

Hartley, Dorothy; *Medieval Costume*, 1993

Hill, Georgina; *History of English Dress from Saxon period to the present day* (2 vols.), 1893

Hole, Christina; *English Folk Lore*, 1947

Hoskins, W. G.; *The Midland Peasant*, 1965

Kalm, Peter; *Account of his visit to England on his way to America*, 1748

Kay, John; Series of English Portraits (Scotland), 1838

Leather, Ella M.; *The Folk-lore of Herefordshire*, 1912

Llanover, Lady; *Welsh Costume and Customs*: The National Library of Wales Picture Book, No. 1, 1951-58

Lodge, M. and Green, R.; *A looking Glass on London*, 1594, 1930 ed.

McClintock, H. F.; *Old Irish and Highland Dress*, 1943

Martin, E. W.; *The Secret People – English Village Life After 1754*, 1954

Maxwell, Stuart and Hutchinson, R.; *Scottish Costume*, 1958

National Library of Wales; *Welsh Costume*

Planché, J. R.; *A Cyclopaedia of Costume*, 1876-79

Planché, J. R.; *Library of Entertaining Knowledge*, 1884

Pyne, W. H.; *The Costume of Great Britain*, 1808

Roberts, Peter; *The Cambrian Popular Antiquities*, 1815

Scot, Reginald; *A Perfect Performance in a Hop Garden*, 1574

Smith, J. T.; *Cries of London*, 1810

Speed, John; *The Theatre of the Empire of Great Britain*, 1611

Strutt, Joseph; *A complete View of the Dress and Habits of the People of England*, 1796

Strutt, Joseph; *Manners and Costume*, 1775

Taylor, T.; *Welch Peasantry*, 1804

Traill & Mann; *English Social History*, 1901-4

Trevelyan, G. M.; *English Social History* (illus. Edition), 1949-52

Trinity College, Dublin; Book of Kells

Tusser, Thomas; *Five Hundred Pointes of good Husbandrie*, 1573

Victoria and Albert Museum; Braun, Georgius and Hogenberg, Franz: *Civitates Orbis Terrarum*, 1572-1618, 1612 ed.
Holkham Bible, 14th C.
Winchester Bible, 12th C.

Walker, George; *The Costume of Yorkshire*, 1814

Walker, J. C.; *Historical Essay on the Dress of the Ancient and Modern Irish*, 1787

Wills, Barclay; *Shepherds of Sussex*, 1938 ed.

Worlidge, John; *Systema Agriculturae*, 1669, 1675

Young, A.; *Annals of Agriculture: a six weeks' tour through the Southern Counties of England and Wales,* 1772

ICELAND

Blöndal and Sigtrygsson; *General Islandsk Kultur i Billider,* 1929

ITALY

Azzerboni, Giuseppe; *Peasant Costume,* 1790

Bernades, D. de; *Costume,* 1815
Boilly, Jules; *Collection des costumes Italiens,* 1827 8
Bosa; *Costume des Venitiens,* 19th C.
Bosq, Eugenio; *Italian Costume,* 1827
Bosq, Eugenio; *Collections des Costumes de Trieste,* early 19th C.

Pinelli, B.; *Nuova Raccollado di Cinquante Costumi,* 1823

Studio, The (Editor Charles Holme); *Peasant Art in Italy,* 1913

Toesca, E. Barti (publisher of Ms.); *Tacuinum Sanitatis,* late 14th C.
Toesca Pietro; *L'Ufiziolo Visconteo Landau-Finaly,* 1951

Vecellio, Cesare; Costume Engravings, 1590
Vico, Enea; Engravings, 1558

Waterhouse; *Baroque Painting in Rome,* 1937

MALTA

Luke, Sir Harry; *Malta,* 1960
Maltese Folklore Review, Vol. 1, No. 3. Malta, 1966

NETHERLANDS

Bing, Val. & van Ueberfeldt, Braet; *Nederlands klederdrachten naar de natuur getekeend,* 1857
Blink, Dr. A.; *Opkomst en ontwickkeling van den Boerenstand*

de Bree, J.; *Bijdragen tot de kennis der Klederdrachten in Zeeland en haar onderling verband van tot heden* (1st en 2de Stuk), 1954
Duyvetter, J. & van Thienen, F. W. S.; *Klederdrachten,* 1962
Duyvetter, J.; *Noord en Zuid Nederlandse Volkskunst*

Gardilanne, G. de, Moffat, Helen and Oakes, Alma; *National Costume of the Netherlands,* 1932

Giucciardini; *Paissi Bassi*, 16th C.

Groen, Ivan der; *Den Nederlandse Hoevenier*, 1670

Kinderen-Besir, Meirvid; *Mode Metamorphosen de Kleedij onzer Voorouders in de 16ce eeuw*, 1933

Maaskamp, E.; *Afbeeldingen van de Kleeding*, 1803, 1808

Nederland door de Eeuwenheen; *Atlas van Stolk*

Rijksmuseum, Print Room; van den Berge, Piet, 18th C.

van den Boerenstand; "Nederland door de Eeuwenheen," vol. 17

van Hinte, Dr. J.; *Een Nederlands Nederzetting in Danemark*, Leiden, 1938

van Urk, Mariap; Urk, Island of (Ms.)

Zeeuws Museum, Middelburg; Nicholas Visser (copied by S. S. Snijders), 1787

NORWAY

Lexow, Einar; *Norske Folksdragter* (illus. J. F. S. Dreiers), Kristiania, 1913

Tonsberg, Christian; *Norske Nationaldragter*, 1892

Unesco Wold Art; *Paintings from the Stave Churches*, 1955

SPAIN AND PORTUGAL

Ackermann; *World in Miniature: Spain and Portugal*, 1826

A.P.D.G.; *Sketches of Portuguese Life*, 1826

(British Museum); *Album Amicorum*, 1623-25

Leveque; *Costumes de Portugal*, 1814

Palencia; *E Trage Regional de Espana*, 1926

Unesco World Art; *Romanesque Paintings*, 1957

Weiditz, C.; *Das Trachtenbuch des Christoph Weiditz von seinen Reisen nach Spanien 1529 und der Niederlanden 1531-2*, 1927

SWEDEN

Forssell; *Eet ar i Sverige*, 1827

Nordeska Museet; *Svenska Folkenalsder*, 1923

Svenson; *Skåne Folkdraktor,* 1858

Thulstrup; *Costumes Nationaux Scandinaves,* 1886

SWITZERLAND

Brockmann, Jerosche; *Volksleben,* 1909

Eyries, J. B.; *La Suisse,* 1825

Hierli, J.; *Die Volkstrachten der Ostschweitz;* 1924
Hierli, J.; *Schweizertracht* XVII-XIX *Jahrhunderts,* 1897
Holbein, J.; *Recueil de Costumes,* 1760

Josy, A.; *La Suisse,* 1815

Koenig, F. and Josy, A.; *Costume de Suisse, c.* 1815

Vincent, J. M.; *Costume and Custom in Basle, Berne and Zürich,* 1935

U.S.A.

Earle, Alice Morse; *Costume of Colonial Times,* 1894

Hostetler, John A.; *Amish Life,* 1952

Museums and Libraries

BELGIUM
Brussels: Musée des Beaux Arts, Salle d'Estampes
Ghent: Musée de Sierkunst
   University of Ghent, Archives

DENMARK
Copenhagen: National Museum
   Royal Library
Amager Island: Amager Costume Museum

ENGLAND
Brighton: Public Reference Library
Castle Rising: Trinity Hospital
Chichester: Public Library
Hereford: Museum
Lincoln: Usher Art Gallery
London: British Museum
   Courtauld Institute (de Witt Collection)
   Victoria and Albert Museum
   Wellington Museum
Oxford: Bodleian Library (Douce Collection, 1830)

NETHERLANDS
Amsterdam: Rijksmuseum
Arnhem: Rijksmuseum voor Volkskunde Het Nederlands Openlucht-
   museum
Middelburg: Zeeuws Museum
Utrecht: Bischoplijk Museum

NORWAY
Oslo: Norsk Folkmuseum

SCOTLAND
Edinburgh: National Museum of Antiquities

WALES
Aberystwyth: National Library of Wales
Cardiff: Welsh Folk Museum, St. Fagans

Index

Entries in italic type refer to illustrations

Breton coif, 49: *88*

Breughel, 39, 49, 215: *17-27, 96, 98, 99, 102, 103, 218, 219, 337, 341-4, 362*

BREVIARY OF PHILIPPE LE BON, 135, 163

Bride's dress, 113, 168: *152:*bridal crown, 166-7

Brogues, 150, 153, 198

Brome, J., 105, 201

Brown, Ivor, 202

Buckles, 81, 82, 151-3, 191, 211

Butler, Samuel, 143

Buttons, 31, 123, 139, 143, 160, 165, 166, 198, 202, 211: *52*

Calash-hood, 101

Cap, 17, 88, 89, 175, 189, 191, 193, 198, 202, 203, 208: *26, 51, 196, 317-61:* sherman's tasselled, 17, 31; mob cap, 189, Saxon, 17, 19, 21, 31, 47, 49, 67

Cape, 21, 31, 77, 79, 93-105: shoulder, 17

CAPUTUM, 193

CAPUZE, 99

Cardiff Museum, 210, 212

Cardigan, Lord and Lady, 103

Cardinal cloak, 103, 202, 216

CASAQUE (CASAWEKE), 139

Cassock, 109

Cawfield and Sawold, 146

Celtic Irish mantle, *see* Irish mantle

Charles, B. G., 206

Chatelaine, 165, 181

Chaucer, Geoffrey, 156, 173, 218, 221

CHEMISE, *241*

CHEMISETTE, 59, 61, 69, 72, 117

Chin clout, 179, 217: *234*

CHITON, 15, 133, 195

Chomes, Noel, 157

CHOPPINO, 45, 152, 155, 158, 217,

Cloak, 17, 29, 43, 45, 63, 77, 79, 81, 90, 93-105, 111, 135, 175, 198, 199, 204, 207, 210-11: *1, 164, 165, 173, 180, 182-4, 194, 196, 198, 200:* Cardinal, 103, 202, 216; Hereford, 103; hooded, 15, 17, 19, 21, 31, 77, 79, 90, 103, 105, 107, 175, 189, 198, 199, 207: *197;* Munster, 103, 199: scarlet, 103, 108, 187, 193, 216: *200;* straw, *183*

Clogs, 31, 81, 153, 155-8, 191, 211: clogging, 157, 158; dances, 158

Coat, 109, 121, 141, 191, 198, 201, 202, 205, 208, 211, 219: *51, 52, 59, 182:*

bourgeois sleeveless, *39;* redingote, *38;* sheepskin, *61;* short bourgeois type, *66*

Cochineal, 21, 216

Cochull brat, 195

Cockers, 158-9, 217

Coif, 19, 47, 49, 63, 65, 67, 73, 77, 82-91, 160, 175, 177, 179, 181, 183, 185, 189, 191, 193, 198, 200-2, 211, 212, 217: *91, 114, 139, 223:* bands, 87-8; Breton, 49: *88;* conical, 86, 88; "floating", 65, 83; "flounced", *193;* fur, 21, 29, 31; HENIN, *see* separate entry; LIRRIPIPE-type, *103;* pointed and shaped, 49; Saxon, 17, 19, 21, 31, 47, 49; seamen's, 21; starched, 47, 86, 87; Volendam, 21: *128;* winged, 85, 86, 183; wimple-type, 47, 49: *101, 159*

Collar, 27, 41, 61, 69, 79, 95, 103, 105, 108, 109, 117, 119, 123, 135, 137, 139, 141, 143, 145-7, 169, 177, 179, 183, 187, 189, 197, 198, 200, 201, 205: *290*

Constable, John, 146

Cords, 135, 139, 173

Corn-holding cloths, 164: *4, 267*

Corot, 167: *255*

Corsage, 181, 202, 208: *139, 216, 299*

Corset, 59, 117, 119, 121, 123: *115, 216, 253, 254, 299*

Corset-bodice, 41, 43, 59, 61, 67, 69, 72, 75, 115-32, 160, 167, 179, 189, 191: *145, 243-5, 252*

COTE, 39, 133, 206, 218

"Cote Hardie" kirtle, 173

Creel, fish, 203-5

CREPIDA, 148

CRESPIGNE ring, 65

Crome, John, 146

Cross cloth, *331*

Cuffs, 137, 139, 141, 143, 147, 189, 198, 202, 204, 205: starched, 47

Cummerbund, 47, *48, 56*

Cunnington, C. H., 15, 101, 162, 195, 217

Cylindrical headgear, 85, 86, 88

Davenport, Mila, 117

De Bruyn, 167: *31*

De Gardilanne, Gracianne, 125, 141

De Heere, Lucas, 108, 109, 125, 164, 179, 181: *286*